Oslo 26/5 04

Happy Cooking!

Best.

Lars Erik Underthun

The Norwegian Culinary Team and Bengt Wilson

NORWAY ON A PLATE

A modern, Norwegian cook book

Written by Wenche Tømt

All foodpictures: Bengt Wilson
Other pictures: Per Eide, Bengt Wilson, Dole Norum, Husmo foto
Translated by: Melody Favish
Pecipes: The Norwegian Culinary Team
Layout: Dole
Grafic total production: Tangen Grafiske Senter AS

All rights reserved. No part of this publication may be reproduced or
transmitted in any form or by any means without written permission of the copyright owner.
All applications regarding this book can be made to: Bengt Wilson AS, Marstrandgaten 13, 0566 OSLO, NORWAY.

To Lovers of Good Food Everywhere

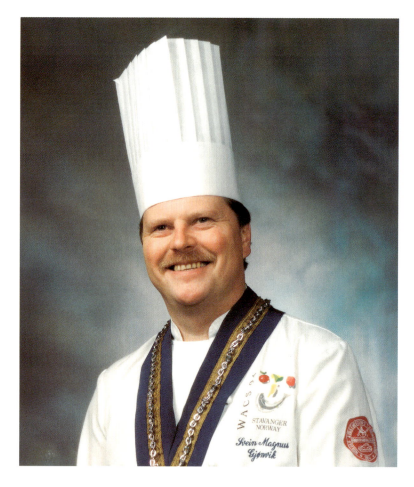

In this book, the members of the Norwegian Culinary Team present some of the best our national kitchen has to offer, our own unique food culture. When I say culture, I know very well that I can use this expression to describe what we chefs do, either during competitions or at our work everyday.

There's no doubt that food is culture - on the same level as music, theater or other artistic presentations. One definition of culture is that a picture of the country's character and history can be expressed through visual or other understandable forms. We chefs do this through the foundation for our existence - food. Without food, our society would not survive; without food, people could not develop. Food reveals the special character of a country, through flavor, preparation, visual presentation, and not least, the use of each country's natural products. In other words, the chef is a purveyor of culture.

On behalf of the Norwegian Chefs' Association and the Norwegian Culinary Team, I would like to extend my greetings to all users of this book. I hope you will gain some insight into the traditions and dishes we have in Norway. Through the use of traditional ingredients, the members of the Culinary Team make modern Norwegian food. They have used their artistic talents to create the finest dishes with the best ingredients we have.

I would like to thank all our supporters and partners who have made this book possible. They have help to lay the foundation for the Norwegian Culinary Team's success, through their understanding and support of our work.

Good luck to those of you who will use this book and to the Norwegian Culinary Team with future challenges and competitions.

The Norwegian Chefs' Association

Svein Magnus Gjønvik

CONTENTS

TO LOVERS OF GOOD FOOD EVERYWHERE	2
TRADITIONAL INGREDIENTS - MODERN FOOD	4
FINNMARK	6
TOR MORTEN MYRSETH	8
GRILLED MARINATED SALMON WITH MUSTARD SAUCE	10
SALT-BAKED COD WITH BEET SAUCE	12
SALMON SOUP WITH PICKLED ROOT VEGETABLES	14
BAKED DRIED SALT COD WITH SMOKED TOMATOES	16
BAKED REINDEER STRIP LOIN WITH THYME	18
DRIED SALT COD PIZZA	20
CLOUDBERRY MOUSSE CAKE	22
LOFOTEN	24
ODD IVAR SOLVOLD	26
HEARTY COD AND TOMATO BOUILLON	28
CREAMY FISH AND SHELLFISH SOUP	29
LUKEWARM JARLSBERG TART	30
COD AND OCEAN CRAYFISH PIZZA	32
POLLACK AND POTATOES LAYERED WITH ONION MARMALADE	34
HERBED RACK OF LAMB WITH MARINATED EGGPLANT	36
SEMI-FROZEN APPLE-SPICE CREAM WITH CANDIED APRICOTS	38
TRØNDELAG	40
LARS LIAN	42
ERICHSEN´S NUT CAKE	44
CAPPUCCINO ICE CREAM CAKE	46
STRAWBERRY CAKE	48
FRUITCAKE	50
ALMOND MACAROON CAKE	52
PASJONS FRUIT MOUSSE	54
ALMOND RING CAKE	56
FJORD NORWAY	58
FRANK BAER	60
SALMON BURGERS WITH SMOKED JARLSBERG	62
SALMON WITH HERB RISOTTO	64
MARINATED SALMON SANDWICH	66
LIGHTLY SALTED AND SMOKED LEG OF LAMB	68
BAKED HALIBUT	70
BACALAO SUPERIORE	72
WARM CHERRIES WITH RED WINE SAUCE AND CINNAMON ICE CREAM	74
ROGALAND	76
HARALD OSA	78
LIGHTLY-SALTED COD AND SMOKED SHRIMP WITH ALMOND POTATO PUREE	80
BROCHETTES OF SALMON AND HALIBUT IN SOY SAUCE MARINADE	82
SHRIMP IN THEIR SHELLS WITH HERB SAUCE AND TOAST	84
SARDINES ON TOAST	86
HERBED LAMB FILET WITH AROMATIC VEGETABLES	88
BACON, ONION AND JARLSBERG QUICHE	90
COLD RHUBARB-STRAWBERRY SOUP	91
SØRLANDET	92
TROND MOI	94
PICKLED MACKEREL WITH SUMMER VEGETABLES	96
MACKEREL BURGERS WITH COLD RHUBARB SOUP	98
BAKED HALIBUT WITH LEMON THYME SAUCE	100
SALAD WITH SMOKED JARLSBERG CHEESE AND MARINATED EGGPLANT	102
FILET OF VEAL WITH ROSEMARY AND JARLSBERG SCALLOPED POTATOES	104
HADDOCK QUENELLES WITH CURRIED JARLSBERG SAUCE	106
VEILED SOUTHERN GIRLS	108
17TH OF MAY	110
NINA SJØEN	112
17TH OF MAY CAKE	114
PASJONS FRUIT CHEESECAKE	116
ANISE PARFAIT	118
BAKED APPLES IN FILO	120
WARM CHOCOLATE TART WITH COCONUT SAUCE	122
AUTUMN TARTE	123
NORWEGIAN COOKIES	124
RØROS	126
JØRN LIE	128
BARBEQUE-SMOKED TROUT	130
SALMON SCHNITZEL WITH OYSTER TARTAR	132
PASTRY LAYERS WITH JARLSBERG CHEESE AND MARINATED TOMATOES WITH BASIL	134
SMOKED SALMON CREAM WITH A SALAD AND VEGETABLES	136
SMOKED SALMON WITH FRIED QUAIL EGGS AND MUSTARD SAUCE	138
DRIED MEATS WITH JARLSBERG CHEESE	140
CHOCOLATE TERRINE WITH PLUM COMPOTE	142
WINTER NORWAY	144
YNGVAR NILSEN	146
ROAST PTARMIGAN BREAST AND REINDEER FILET WITH LINGONBERRY SAUCE	148
OCEAN CRAYFISH SOUP	150
SAFFRON MUSSEL TART	152
GRILLED SCALLOPS WITH CELERIAC PUREE AND RED WINE SAUCE	154
GRILLED DRIED SALT COD WITH VICHY-CARROTS AND BACON	156
HADDOCK STEW	158
LIME SOUFFLÉ WITH BLACKBERRY SAUCE	159
INDEX	160

Traditional ingredients – Modern food

Norway is a country of fjords, mountains and beautiful scenery. It is rich in the products of the fields, forests and sea, with game and excellent fish and shellfish. With our long, light summer nights, pristine seas and special climatic conditions thanks to the Gulf Stream, Norway has some of the best ingredients in the world.

For chefs, ingredients will always be of primary importance. The only way to prepare top-quality food is to use top-quality ingredients. When we travel abroad, we take our ingredients with us. We want to draw special attention to the quality of our fish and shellfish. Off our long coastline, growing conditions are excellent for firm-fleshed, flavorful fish. And our dairy products are in a class all their own. Once you get used to Norwegian butter and cream, it takes a lot of convincing to go over to anything else. Their flavors and uses are unlimited.

This book is based on Norwegian ingredients when they are best. Some products are used year-round, while others have their special seasons. The kitchen should follow the seasons for the pleasure of the person standing at the stove as well as that of the guests. Strawberries in December are just not right. You will find many traditional Norwegian products in our recipes, and Norwegian cuisine is always in the forefront. But you won't find "Grandmother's cooking" in NORWAY ON A PLATE. We want you to become familiar with the new Norwegian cuisine. All of us on the Norwegian Culinary Team hope that our book will give pleasure and inspiration to all who appreciate good food.

with culinary greetings

The Norwegian Culinary Team

FINNMARK
- exotic, different, full of flavors

Where would most Norwegians like to go on vacation? According to surveys, which do not take cost into consideration, the answer is: As far north as we can get in our own country! That's not really so unusual - Finnmark has a lot to offer!

Norwegian traditions
In Alta, there are rare stone age rock carvings, which are on the UNESCO cultural heritage list. The snow-clad peaks in the distance and the beautiful Alta fjord contribute to a magical feeling - this is an exciting world to explore. And there are beautiful valleys, too. With the serenity of the wilderness on all sides, visitors can stay at farms and guest houses. They can sit around a fire, enjoy a sauna and a comfortable bed after a day spent outdoors. This region is home to moose, wolverines, and hares, and you might even see a lynx or a bear.

True Finnmark food is reindeer, prepared in countless ways - in bouillon, tongue, marrow bones, filet, roasts and chops. But there's also ptarmigan, salmon and freshwater fish from mountain lakes. And the favorite dessert? Cloudberries, of course.

More surprising. There's a vineyard in Lakselv, which produces fortified crowberry which has received good reviews. Nordkapp wine tastes of heather and open country, and it's going to be our northernmost county's newest export, if the producer has anything to do with it.

The preservation of fish is an art up here. That's not unusual, considering the long shoreline and the many clear mountain lakes in the region. Smoking, curing, salting and drying - all are methods of preserving fish so it will keep longer. And there are ingenious methods of preparing fish as well.

-The sea may be greedy, but it's also generous, say the people of these parts. It has taken many a life, but it has saved many more. And even in the northernmost town in the world, Hammerfest, there are restaurants serving good food with roots in the regional traditions.

Sami tradition
At the Sami center in Karasjok is a permanent exhibition featuring Sami culture and traditions, with silversmith, knife smith, crafts and textiles. Sami culture is blossoming, especially in Karasjok and Kautokeino. Tourism is becoming more and more important for the economy of this region, where Sami, Norwegians and Finns live side by side. Up here, leisure and recreational possibilities are enormous and exotic. There's the wide plateau, with rivers and lakes...
But back to the reindeer. Beloved children have many names. The word "reindeer" comes from the Old Norse "hreinn" which derives

from the Germanic "hraia," which means horned animal. There are about 6.5 million reindeer in the world today. About 60% of these are tame, farmed animals. Managing the reindeer requires the kind of knowledge and ability all indigenous peoples (such as the Sami) need to survive, the Sami say themselves.

The Finnmark plateau is especially wonderful in the autumn - when the landscape is ablaze with red and yellow leaves, and the Sami herd and corral their flocks after summer grazing. Some of the animals are slaughtered, while others are kept over the winter. Sami women have their own animals, and children are given reindeer as christening and confirmation gifts.

In Karasjok, there is an excellent restaurant. At "Storgammen," up to 100 guests can be served in the large "lavvo" (tent), which was built according to Sami tradition. The open flames crackle and send sparks over the stone floor. Guests dine off wooden trays placed on tree stumps in front of their reindeer-skin covered seats. They are then served boiled meat, specialties made with blood and the strongest bouillon in the world - all made from reindeer, of course.

But - come with us to modern Finnmark - with flavorful, new dishes - based on the best products from the "Arctic kitchen" and with the best traditions as a departure point.

Name:
 Tor Morten Myrseth
DOB:
 January 11, 1965
Present Position:
 Chef de cuisine, Frognerseteren Restaurant, Oslo.
Previous Positions:
 Cook, Hotel Stefan, Oslo; Cook, Brasserie Landholt, Geneva; souschef and later chef at Hotel Stefan. A number of assignments for the Norwegian Export Council to promote Norwegian seafood abroad. Has worked for Intercontinental Hotels, USA - New York, Miami, Washington - with fish and shellfish.
Awards:
 In addition to awards with the Norwegian Culinary Team: Game chef of the year 1993;
 Silver - Fish chef of the year 1993.

TOR MORTEN MYRSETH
- and his Norwegian country kitchen

High up over Oslo, with a fantastic view of the city and the fjord, is Frognerseteren Restaurant. This old, beautiful log building is an Oslo landmark, surrounded by many walking and skiing trails. The apple cake here is famous. But there are all kinds of Norwegian specialties in chef Tor Morten Myrseth's kitchen.

Do you have a food philosophy?

It has to be to preserve the natural flavor of our ingredients. It's a question of searching for combinations which accentuate the flavors of the individual ingredients. I also like to use the seasons actively in my kitchen. All products are best in their natural season.

What do you have to say about Norwegian products?

We are the best in the world when it comes to fish, shellfish, game, fruit and berries. In our cold climate, with its long growing time. the flavors of the products develop to their highest potential! Norwegian butter and cream are excellent. But I'd like better quality potatoes.

What is your favorite dish?

It depends on the time and the occasion. My wife Anne's pizza is a favorite. Otherwise, it has to be fish and shellfish dishes.

Do you have your own style in the kitchen?

It's based on Norwegian ingredients and follow the seasons. I like to compose dishes in both traditional and non-traditional ways, or for that matter - to combine them. I emphasize purity in my presentation of food - always from its best side. It's a combination of French and Norwegian, old and new. Flavor is always the most important, but the food has to look good, too.

Why did you become a chef?

Ever since I was a child, I've gone fishing with my grandfather. Afterwards, we always prepared our catch. Since then, I always wanted to be a chef. I like challenges, and there are plenty of them here. Even just balancing the flavor with the visual is an art! It is also exciting to preserve our old traditions - such as salting, curing, smoking, etc.

Do you have time for any other interests?

I work out a bit. In my profession, you have to keep in shape. I like to spend my free time with my wife Anne and my family, go to my cabin and fish. And, of course, I have my motorcycle...

What is the most important thing for you?

I am best when I like what I do and am satisfied with the results. Then, it's easier to be creative and to be there for those around me, both at home and on the job, to contribute in a positive way.

What kind of food do you make in your home kitchen?

It varies. Everything from pizza to simple and fancier shellfish and fish dishes. Some Swiss dishes, such as cheese fondue and raclette, also appear on our table. And food from the East...

Any thoughts about the future?

As far as food is concerned, I hope and believe that we will concentrate on using seasonal products and maintain the purity of Norwegian ingredients. As a whole, we will make purer food.

Grilled Marinated Salmon with Mustard Sauce

- 4 servings -

*1 kg (2 1/4 lbs) boneless
but not skinless salmon fillet
50 g (4 tablespoons, 1/4 cup) sugar
50 g (2 1/2 tablespoons) salt
1/4 teaspoon freshly ground white pepper
2 tablespoons chopped fresh dill*

It is also possible to use purchased marinated salmon (gravlaks) in this dish. Count on 100 g (4 oz) per person.

Mustard sauce:
*50 g (1/3 cup) chopped shallots
1 tablespoon butter
8 dl (3 1/3 cups) fish stock
5 white peppercorns
2 bay leaves
6 dl (2 1/2 cups) whipping cream
1 tablespoon Dijon mustard
1 tablespoon whole grain mustard
salt and pepper*

Dill coulis:
*4 tablespoons (1/4 cup)
coarsely chopped fresh dill
1 dl (scant 1/2 cup) olive oil
1 1/2 teaspoons lemon juice
1/2 teaspoon salt
1/4 teaspoon freshly ground white pepper
1/2 teaspoon sugar*

Potatoes:
*400 g (14 oz) almond (
or other waxy) potatoes
1 tablespoon vegetable oil
1 tablespoon butter
salt and pepper*

Remove any small bones down the center of the fillet. Place in a glass dish just large enough to hold. Combine sugar, salt and pepper and sprinkle all over the exposed fish meat. Sprinkle with dill. Cover with plastic wrap and refrigerate 3-4 days, turning the fish once a day.

When the salmon is ready, cut into rectangular pieces (about 100 g, 4 oz each) and remove the skin. Once prepared in this way, the fish is ready to grill, about 2 minutes per side.

Mustard sauce: Sauté the shallots in butter about 4 minutes, until soft but not brown. Add stock, peppercorns and bay leaves and bring to a boil. Skim, then reduce over high heat until half the original amount remains. Add cream and reduce again by half. Beat in both kinds of mustard. Season with salt and pepper.

Dill coulis: Blanch the dill in boiling water about 30 seconds. Remove with a slotted spoon and plunge immediately into ice water. Drain. Place in a food processor with the oil and puree 3 minutes, to a smooth, green oil. Season to taste with lemon juice, salt, pepper and sugar.

Potatoes: Peel and dice (1/2 cm, 1/4 in) the potatoes. Fry in oil and butter until golden brown on all sides. Season with salt and pepper.

To serve: Arrange the potatoes on four dinner plates. Top with grilled salmon. Spoon mustard sauce around the fish and drizzle dill coulis here and there over the sauce. Garnish with fresh herbs.

Salt-Baked Cod with Beet Sauce

- 4 servings -

800-900 g (1 3/4 - 2 lbs) boneless but not skinless cod fillet
200 g (1 3/4 dl, 3/4 cup) sea salt
1 tablespoon chopped fresh thyme
1 tablespoon butter

Beet sauce:
50 g (1/3 cup) chopped shallots
butter
4 dl (1 2/3 cups) fish stock
5 white peppercorns
1 1/2 teaspoons chopped fresh thyme
2 bay leaves
4 dl (1 2/3 cups) red wine
100 g (4 oz, 2 small) beets
salt and pepper
1 teaspoon cornstarch dissolved in
1 teaspoon cold water
1 tablespoon chopped chives

250 g (8 oz) slab bacon
water

Vegetables:
100 g (4 oz, 1/4 medium) celeriac
100 g (4 oz, 1/4 small) rutabaga
100 g (4 oz, 3 small) parsley roots
100 g (4 oz, 2 small) carrots
100 g (4 oz, 3-4) scallions

Preheat the oven to 150C (300F). Scale the fish, rinsing well. Cut into 4 rectangular pieces. Arrange a bed of seasalt on a baking tray. Place the fish, skin, side down, on the salt. Bake 10 minutes. Transfer to a platter. Carefully remove the salt. Just before serving, dip the fish in fresh thyme. Sauté, skin side down in butter about 3 minutes.

Beet sauce: Sauté shallots in butter about 4 minutes, until soft but not brown. Add stock, peppercorns, thyme and bay leaves and bring to a boil. Skim well. Reduce over high heat until about 2 dl (3/4 cup) remains. Add red wine and reduce until about 5 dl (2 cups) remain. Strain.
Peel and cut the beet into 1 cm (1/2 in) cubes. Add to the sauce. Simmer until beets are tender, 6-8 minutes. Season with salt and pepper. Thicken with cornstarch, if desired. Fold in the chives.

Place the bacon in a saucepan and add water just to cover. Bring to a boil, lower heat and simmer about 45 minutes. Remove and cut into small slices (1x4 cm, 1/2x1 1/2 in). Reserve cooking liquid.

Vegetables: Clean/peel and wash all vegetables. Cut the root vegetables into batons (1/2x5 cm, 1/4x2 in) and the scallions into 5 cm (2 in) lengths. Cook in the bacon water until tender. Heat the bacon bits in the water just before serving. Drain well.

To serve: Arrange vegetables and bacon on four dinner plates. Top with the fish. Spoon sauce all around and garnish with fresh herbs.

Salmon Soup with Pickled Root Vegetables

– 4 servings –

50 g (1/3 cup) chopped shallots
1 tablespoon butter
1 liter (quart) fish stock
8 peppercorns
4 bay leaves
1 1/2 teaspoons chopped fresh dill
4 dl (1 2/3 cups) dry white wine
1 liter (quart) whipping cream
2 tablespoons flour shaken in a jar with 2 tablespoons water
salt and pepper

Vegetables:
50 g (2 oz, small chunk) celeriac
50 g (2 oz, 1 small) carrot
50 g (2 oz, small chunk) rutabaga
3 dl (1 1/4 cups) water
1 dl (scant 1/2 cup) 7% white vinegar
300 g (10 oz, 3 1/2 dl, 1 1/2 cups) sugar

Sour cream topping:
2 dl (3/4 cup) dairy sour cream (do not use low-fat)
2 teaspoons grated horseradish
1 tablespoon chopped chives
salt and pepper

In a large soup pot, sauté shallots in butter about 4 minutes, until soft but not brown. Add stock, peppercorns, bay leaves and dill and bring to a boil. Reduce over high heat to about 5 dl (2 cups). Add white wine and reduce to about 5 dl (2 cups). Add cream and bring to a boil. Reduce to about 1 liter (quart). The soup can be thickened with flour, if desired. Season with salt and pepper, then strain into a clean pot.

Vegetables:
Peel and wash vegetables. Cut into 1/2 cm (1/4 in) dice. Bring water, vinegar and sugar to a boil. Add vegetables. Remove from the heat and cool the vegetables in the brine. Remove with a slotted spoon. (The brine can be reused many times.)

Sour cream topping: Whip the sour cream (it thins out first, then peaks). Fold in horseradish and chives. Season with salt and pepper.

To serve: Bring the soup to a boil. Add the pickled vegetables. Form the sour cream topping into "eggs" with two tablespoons. Ladle the soup into deep bowls and top with sour cream "eggs." Garnish with fresh herbs.

BAKED DRIED SALT COD WITH SMOKED TOMATOES
– 4 SERVINGS –

400 g (14 oz) dried salt cod
freshly ground pepper

4 ripe tomatoes
2 tablespoons aromatic wood chips (can be purchased at fish markets)

CHILE OIL:
1 dl (1/3 cup) walnut oil
1/2 dl (2 1/2 tablespoons) chile powder
1/4 dl (4 teaspoons) ground cinnamon

SAUCE:
50 g (1/3 cup) coarsely chopped onion
100g (2/3 cup) coarsely chopped ginger
100 g (3 1/2 oz, scant 1/2 cup) unsalted butter
6 dl (2 1/2 cups) hearty fish stock
6 white peppercorns
6 dl (2 1/2 cups) whipping cream
salt and pepper
1 tablespoon flour shaken in a jar with 1 tablespoon water

VEGETABLES:
3 scallions
1 small eggplant
1 tablespoon butter
6 canned plum tomatoes
salt and pepper
2 tablespoons chopped chives
6 almond (or other small waxy) potatoes
1 tablespoon olive oil

Soak the dried salt cod in cold water 4 days, changing water daily. The fish should have increased to at least twice its original size/weight. Then refrigerate 24 hours.

Smoked tomatoes: Cut an "x" at the stem end of each tomato. Dip in boiling water about 30 seconds. Transfer immediately with a slotted spoon to ice water. Peel and quarter. Remove seeds carefully with a spoon. Place on a rack which fits in a pot. Place the pot on the stove over high heat. Sprinkle wood chips over the bottom of the pot and turn on the exhaust fan. Place the tomatoes on the rack, cover and smoke about 5 minutes. Remove from the pot and set aside.

CHILE OIL: Combine all ingredients. Heat gradually to about 60C (140F). (Check with an instant-read thermometer.) Cool, then strain. Store in a jar with a tight lid.

SAUCE: Sauté onion and ginger in butter about 3 minutes, until soft but not brown. Add stock and peppercorns, bring to a boil, then skim. Reduce over high heat to about 2 dl (3/4 cup). Add cream and reduce to 5 dl (2 cups). Strain into a new, clean saucepan. Season with salt and pepper. Thicken with flour, if desired.

VEGETABLES: Clean the scallion and cut into 4 cm (1 1/2 in) lengths. If the eggplant is small and young, do not peel. Cut the eggplant into 1 cm (1/2 in) cubes. Place vegetables in cold water. Melt the butter in a saucepan and add the tomatoes. Simmer, stirring often to make a thick tomato sauce. Drain vegetables and add. Bring to a boil, lower the heat and simmer 2-3 minutes. Season with salt and pepper, then stir in the chives.

Scrub, but do not peel the potatoes. Thinly slice, then toss with cold oil. Heat a "krumkake" or pizelle iron (sold at specialty stores) and brush with oil. Overlap the potato slices on the iron to make a circle. Cook until golden.

FISH: Preheat the oven to 180C (350F). Drain the fish and remove all skin and bones. Cut into four pieces of equal size (about 200 g, 6-7 oz) each and place on a greased baking sheet. Grind pepper over the fish. Bake 15 minutes.

TO SERVE: Arrange the vegetables in tomato sauce on 4 dinner plates. Place the fish on the vegetables, then top with smoked tomatoes. Spoon warm ginger sauce all around and drizzle with chile oil. Serve the potatoes alongside.

Baked Reindeer Strip Loin with Thyme
– 4 servings –

1 kg (2 lbs) reindeer strip loin
1 tablespoon butter
2 tablespoons chopped fresh thyme
salt and pepper

LINGONBERRY SAUCE:
200 g (7 oz, about 3 dl, 1 1/4 cups) mirepoix (equal parts chopped onion, leek, celeriac and carrot)
1 tablespoon butter
6 dl (2 1/2 cups) rich game stock
4 dl (1 2/3 cups) red wine
200 g (7 oz, about 3 dl, 1 1/4 cups) lingonberries
salt and pepper
2 teaspoons cornstarch stirred into 2 teaspoons cold water

BLACK CURRANT SAUCE:
200 g (7 oz, about 3 dl, 1 1/4 cups) equal parts chopped onion, leek, celeriac and carrot
1 tablespoon butter
6 dl (2 1/2 cups) rich game stock
4 dl (1 2/3 cups) Port wine
200 g (7 oz, about 3 dl, 1 1/4 cups) black currants
salt and pepper
2 teaspoons cornstarch stirred into 2 teaspoons cold water

VEGETABLES:
300 g (10 oz) almond (or other waxy) potatoes
1 tablespoon chopped parsley
2 tablespoons butter
salt and pepper
2 sheets puff pastry
2 tablespoons flour
1 egg yolk

300 g (10 oz, 1 small) celeriac
2 dl (3/4 cup) whipping cream
salt and pepper

Make the sauces first:

LINGONBERRY SAUCE: Sauté the diced vegetables in butter until golden. Add the stock, bring to a boil and skim. Reduce over high heat to about 3 dl (1 1/4 cups). Add red wine and lingonberries. Reduce to about 4 dl (1 2/3 cups). Strain into a clean saucepan. Bring to a boil and season with salt and pepper. Thicken with cornstarch and water, if desired.

BLACK CURRANT SAUCE: Follow the directions above, but substitute Port wine and black currants for red wine and lingonberries.

VEGETABLES: Preheat the oven to 220C (425F). Wash, peel and grate/shred the potatoes. Press out as much liquid as possible. Mix with parsley. Sauté lightly in butter, but do not brown. Season with salt and pepper. Cool. Roll out the puff pastry on a floured board. Arrange the potato mixture in a sausage shape along one side of each puff pastry sheet. Brush dough edges with egg yolk. Fold over the potato and press with a fork to seal. Place on a parchment covered baking sheet. Brush with egg yolk. Bake about 10 minutes. Slice before serving.

Peel and wash celeriac. Cut into chunks. Cook in unsalted water until soft. Drain, then place in a food processor and puree. With the motor running, pour in the cream. Season with salt and pepper.

MEAT: Preheat the oven to 200C (400F). Trim the meat, removing all membranes. Brown quickly in butter. Rub with thyme, salt and pepper. Place on a baking sheet and roast about 10 minutes. Let rest 10 minutes before slicing and serving.

TO SERVE: Divide the celeriac puree among 4 dinner dishes. Top with slices of reindeer. Place slices of the potato sausage alongside. Spoon both sauces all around and garnish with fresh herbs.

Dried salt Cod Pizza

- 4 servings -

600 g (20 oz) dried salt cod

Crust:
400 g (6 3/4 dl, 2 3/4 cups) flour
15 g (1/2 oz) fresh yeast
salt and pepper
3 1/2 tablespoons olive oil
1 1/2 dl (2/3 cup) water (body temperature)

Filling:
400 g (14 oz, 4 small) tomatoes
200 g (7 oz, 1 small) eggplant
100 g (4 oz, 5-6 slices) bacon
75 g (1/2 cup) chopped shallots
salt and pepper
ground star anise

200 g (4 1/2 dl, 1 3/4 cups) grated Jarlsberg cheese

Soak the salted dried cod in cold water at least 48 hours, preferably more. Drain, dry and remove skin and bones. Cut into 4 pieces of equal size (about 150 g, 5 oz each).

Crust: Place flour, yeast, salt and pepper in a food processor. With the motor running, add oil in a thin stream. Then, carefully add warm water. Process until the dough forms a ball, then wrap in plastic and let rise in a warm place about 1 hour.

Filling:
Cut an "x" at the stem end of each tomato. Dip in boiling water about 30 seconds. Transfer immediately with a slotted spoon to ice water. Peel. Place half in a saucepan with a little melted butter. Mash carefully with a fork while cooking. Reduce over low heat to a thick mass (this takes about 30 minutes), then sieve.
Cut the eggplant into 1 cm (1/2 in) cubes. Cut the bacon into small strips. Quarter remaining tomatoes, seed and dice. Add the bacon to the tomato sauce and simmer 4 minutes. Add shallots, eggplant and tomatoes and cook until soft. Season with salt, pepper and star anise.

Preheat the oven to 200C (400F). Divide the dough into 4 equal parts and roll out. Place on a greased baking sheet. Spoon filling onto the pizzas. Top with a piece of fish. Sprinkle 2/3 of the grated cheese over and around the fish. Bake 12 minutes.

To serve: Remove the pizzas from the oven and top with remaining cheese and a sprinkle of star anise.

CLOUDBERRY MOUSSE CAKE

This cake can be made with raspberries. It will taste good, but it won't taste anything like cloudberries.

SPICE CAKE BASE:
50 g (3 tablespoons) butter
40 g (3 1/2 tablespoons) sugar
1 egg
25 g (3 tablespoons) flour
1 teaspoon ground cinnamon
1/2 teaspoon ground ginger
1/2 teaspoon ground cardamom
1/2 teaspoon ground star anise
1/2 teaspoon ground cloves
40 g (1 dl, scant 1/2 cup) toasted walnuts, ground
50 g (1 3/4 oz, 1/3 cup) semi-sweet chocolate, chopped

CLOUDBERRY MOUSSE:
500 g (1 lb) cloudberries
7 sheets (2 tablespoons powdered) gelatin
3 eggs
170 g (scant 1 cup) sugar
5 dl (2 cups) whipping cream

FRUIT COMPOTE:
4 dl (1 2/3 cups) St. Halvard liqueur (or Dom Benedictine)
1 whole star anise
100 g (4 oz, 2-3 medium) plums
1 orange
50 g (1/3 cup) raspberries
50 g (1/3 cup) blueberries

SAUCE:
2 dl (3/4 cup) red wine
200 g (1 cup) sugar
100 g (1 1/2 dl) black currants

Preheat the oven to 180C (350F). Grease and flour a 22 cm (9 in) springform pan. Beat butter and sugar until light and fluffy. Beat in the egg. Stir in flour and spices, mixing well. Fold in chopped nuts and chocolate. Bake 10 minutes. Cool completely.

CLOUDBERRY MOUSSE: Press the cloudberries through a sieve. There should be about 250 g (9 oz, just over 1 cup) puree. Soak the gelatin sheets in (Sprinkle the powdered gelatin over 3 tablespoons) cold water to soften, about 10 minutes. Beat egg and sugar until light and lemon-colored. Squeeze excess water from the gelatin sheets (disregard for powdered gelatin) and melt gently in the cloudberry puree. Cool somewhat. Fold the egg mixture into the cloudberry puree. Whip the cream and fold into the cloudberry mixture. Spread over the cake in the pan. Refrigerate at least 3 hours, until the mousse has set.

COMPOTE: Bring liqueur and star anise to a boil. Cut plums into wedges, peel and add to the warm liqueur. Cool completely. Cut the orange into sections, removing all membrane. Add to the liqueur mixture along with the berries.

SAUCE: Simmer red wine with sugar and black currants about 10 minutes. Strain and refrigerate 1 hour.

TO SERVE: Arrange pieces of cake on plates and top with marinated fruit. Spoon sauce around the cake.

LOFOTEN
wild and beautiful, cod and lamb

Nordland and the Lofoten islands in the north. Lofoten is one of the places in Norway which attract the most tourists. And the food? Two things come to mind-- cod and Lofoten lamb! You can really find quality ingredients in this wild northern outpost.

THE LANDSCAPE ITSELF IS INSPIRATION,

"The Lofoten mountains have a bluish cast. I don't know what is the more magnificent, either to see them from afar as a deep blue wall with a thousand sentry towers - or to get close and see the wall open up, with every peak becoming a mountain on its own, the one always more fantastic than the other." If we could write like Norway's national poet, we, too, could have expressed ourselves in this way about the fantastic row of peaks lying southwest on the horizon.

We can well understand why mature cod want to come to these waters to spawn. From January through March, the cod come from the Barents Sea. Some say that its delicate white meat, liver and roe give energy and fertility to the people living along the coast. These cod can measure up to 150 cm (5 ft) in length, and they are very lean, only 3% fat.

During the 'sixties, a "rorbu" vacation in the Lofoten Islands became the thing to do. Real live old-fashioned fishing villages with fishermen and fish in the winter, tourists in the summer. Those places, which once were both home and workplace, are now rented out for the short summer season. There are also complexes built for this purpose, modern and convenient. Charming places with the scent of tar and dried fish attract people nowadays.

FROM SEA AND SHORE

The kitchen here in the north is just as varied and many-sided as the landscape itself. Archaeological digs, including those at Borg in Lofoten, show that this area had extensive contact and trade with the continent as early as the eighth century. That's probably one reason why no one's been afraid to use new and strange ingredients to a greater degree than anywhere else in the country. The outgoing, liv-

ely inhabitants combine this with the region's own somewhat non-traditional resources. With a firm anchoring in tasty traditions, new and delicious dishes are being developed all the time.

Or – what do you say about dishes such as filet of lamb marinated in liquor? Lambs and sheep graze right out on the edge of the icy northern sea. They climb the mountains and nibble along the shore. That has to produce good lamb. And true enough--this meat has been voted Norway's best. Almost like the "pre-sale" lamb from Brittany, we've been told. And when the people here get fresh lamb to prepare, they make real Lofoten lamb and barley soup, they marinate filets or they serve a golden brown leg of lamb at Sunday dinner. Or maybe even a real northern Norwegian fish soup?

Cod is and always will be the most important resource up here. A local boy, the poet-priest Peter Dass, once wrote, "If the cod lets us down, what would we have?"

The answer has to be, the "world's best lamb."

Name:
   Odd Ivar Solvold
DOB:
   June 21, 1969
Present Position:
   Souschef, Edgar Ludl's Gourmet, Sandefjord.
Previous Positions:
   Rica Park Hotel, Sandefjord, cook at Edgar Ludl from 1989.
Awards:
   Silver – Chaine des Rotisseurs national competition for young chefs, 1988; Silver – Chaine de Rotisseurs international competition, Nice, 1988; Gold – Chaine de Rotisseurs national competition, 1989; Silver – Norwegian Championships for chefs 1990; Gold – Norwegian Championships for chefs 1991; Gold – Norway's fish chef 1993; Gold and King's Cup – Norwegian Championships for chefs 1993; Gold – Norwegian Championships for chefs 1994; Gold – Nordic team championships 1995. In addition, a number of gold and silver medals with the Norwegian Culinary Team 1990/92 and 1992/96 American Culinary Classic; Salon Culinaire, Singapore; Culinary Olympics, Ika Hoga.

ODD IVAR SOLVOLD
Master of competitions and a dream host

He's been Norwegian champion in cooking more times than anyone else. This young chef thrives like a fish in water when the pressure is greatest in national and international competitions. Solvold is Norway's representative to the World Championship for Chefs (Bocuse d'Or) in Lyon in 1997. Otherwise, you can find him at "Ludls Gourmet" in Sandefjord, a coastal city southwest of Oslo, about 90 minutes by car from Norway's capital.

Tell us about your food philosophy.

The most important thing is to retain the flavors of the individual ingredients. You have to have good ingredients to make top quality food. In that way, we are quite privileged here in Norway, with all our fish and dairy products.
You have to take time to consider all the aspects of an ingredient in order to be able to get the most out of it.

What do you think about Norwegian ingredients?

My departure point is always to use Norwegian ingredients when they are best.
But, I also use "foreign" ingredients when they are better or when they can't be produced in Norway. The kitchen of the future will always be multicultural. In Norway, we never will have a climate for oranges, lemons, etc.
But now, new ingredients are being produced in Norway. This is all right, but I won't say they're the best you can get once they are on the market. Behind every ingredient lie generations of experience and knowledge which can't be learned in a few years.

What are your favorite dishes?

I really don't have any. For me, food is mood-oriented. One day, poached cod with Sandefjord butter (a kind of mousseline sauce) is the best I could imagine, the next, perhaps homemade pizza with tomatoes, Parma ham, fresh basil and a mixture of Jarlsberg and Parmesan.

What about your own cooking style?

My cooking style is as varied as the weather. It changes all the time and is constantly being renewed. This is because I am always seeking new things. I feel like an explorer in the mysteries of ingredients and the cuisines of other cultures.

Why did you become a chef?

I've always been interested in food, traditions and ingredients. I just had to try. And when I got the chance to begin with Edgar Ludl (one of Norway's great master chefs), I knew that I had chosen correctly. To discuss ideas and share a kitchen with a true master has given me both inspiration and professional prowess.

The most important thing for you?

To learn more and develop, both as a chef and as a person. My wife, Elisabeth, is also an accomplished professional chef. We share so much, both on the personal and professional level, and I think that's great.

What about food in your home kitchen?

We don't eat much at home, because we spend most of our time at work. When we do get around to making food at home, we explore the kitchens of other countries using the ingredients we buy on our trips abroad or in international food stores.

The future - for you and for food?

Our producers and suppliers have to become better at selecting ingredients according to quality, and we chefs have to be more conscious of the ingredients we choose throughout the year. In this way, we won't have mediocre ingredients once they are in season. My future won't be very different from the present; a continuous quest for new experiences.

HEARTY COD AND TOMATO BOUILLON

- 4 SERVINGS -

BOUILLON:
4 shallots, peeled and sliced
1 dl (scant 1/2 cup) Noilly Prat
(or dry white wine)
5 dl (2 cups) clear fish stock
300 g (10 oz) boneless and skinless cod fillet
salt

MAYONNAISE:
1 egg yolk
1 tablespoon Dijon mustard
2 garlic cloves, blanched 5 minutes and mashed
1 tablespoon lemon juice
3 dl (1 1/4 cups) walnut oil
chopped fresh basil
salt and freshly ground white pepper

Garnish:
4 tomatoes
salt and freshly ground white pepper

MAYONNAISE: Combine egg yolk, mustard, garlic and lemon juice in a bowl. Mix well. Pour in the oil in a thin stream, whisking constantly, to make a thick mayonnaise. Stir in lots of chopped fresh basil and season with salt and pepper. Store in the refrigerator.

GARNISH: Cut an "x" at the stem end of each tomato. Dip in boiling water about 30 seconds. Transfer immediately with a slotted spoon to ice water. Peel, seed and cut into wedges.
SOUP: Combine shallots and Noilly Prat in a saucepan and reduce until almost no liquid remains. Add fish stock and bring to a boil. Cut the fish into cubes and add. Lower the heat and poach until just cooked through, about 5 minutes. Remove the fish with a slotted spoon and keep warm.
Season the stock to taste with salt and pepper. Add the tomatoes and return to a boil. Return the cod to the pan and heat through.

TO SERVE: Divide the soup and fish among four deep bowls. Top with a spoonful of mayonnaise and garnish with fresh basil leaves.

CREAMY FISH AND SHELLFISH SOUP

- 4 SERVINGS -

2 tablespoons minced shallot
1 tablespoon butter
1 dl (scant 1/2 cup) white wine
4 dl (1 2/3 cups) fish stock
1 star anise
2 dl (7/8 cup) whipping cream

1 small carrot
1 parsley root
200 g (8 oz) monkfish fillet (all lilac membrane removed)
1/2 leek
100 g (4 oz) trout or salmon fillet
4 ocean crayfish

200 g (8 oz) cooked shrimp, shelled
4 teaspoons butter
1 tablespoon chopped fresh chervil
1 tablespoon chopped chives
salt and freshly ground white pepper

Sauté the shallot in butter. Add white wine and reduce over high heat until about half the original amount remains. Add fish stock and star anise and reduce over high heat until about 2 dl (7/8 cup) remains. Add cream and bring to a boil. Season with salt and white pepper.
Peel the carrot and parsley root, cut into chunks and add to the soup. Simmer about 5 minutes. Cut the monkfish into chunks, slice the leek and add. Simmer 5 minutes. Cut the trout into chunks and add. Simmer 4 minutes. Add the crayfish and simmer 3 minutes. Add the shrimp and heat through.

TO SERVE: Divide the fish, vegetables and shellfish among four deep bowls. Add the butter to the soup and mix well with an immersion blender. Add chervil and chives. Pour the warm soup over the fish, etc., just before serving.

Lukewarm Jarlsberg Tart
– 4 servings –

CRUST:
5 dl (2 cups) flour
150 g (5 oz, 10 tablespoons) unsalted butter
1 egg
3 1/2 tablespoons water
pinch salt

FILLING:
5 tablespoons (about 1/3 cup) chopped shallots
2 tablespoons butter
3 eggs
2 dl (7/8 cup) whipping cream
300 g (10 oz, 2 1/2 cups) grated Jarlsberg cheese
cayenne pepper
salt and freshly ground white pepper
2 tablespoons chopped chives

CELERY OIL:
100 g (4 oz) celery (2 small stalks)
5 dl (2 cups) water
2 teaspoons salt
1 dl (scant 1/2 cup) walnut oil
freshly ground white pepper

BELL PEPPER PESTO:
1 red bell pepper
1 tablespoon vegetable oil
salt
1 garlic clove, peeled and blanched 5 minutes
1 dl (1/3 cup) olive oil
salt and freshly ground white pepper
3 tablespoons pine nuts (or chopped walnuts)

GOAT CHEESE CREAM:
100g (4 oz) Snøfrisk cheese (or fresh goat cheese or cream cheese)
1 tablespoon cottage cheese
1 tablespoon chopped chives
salt and freshly ground white pepper

CRUST: Place all ingredients in a food processor and pulse until the dough holds together. Wrap in plastic and refrigerate at least 1 hour. Roll out to 2-3 mm (1/16 in) thick on a floured board. Press into a 24 cm (9 in) tart pan with 3 cm (1 1/4 in) high sides. Trim excess dough.

FILLING: Preheat the oven to 180C (350F). Sauté shallot in butter. Whisk eggs and cream. Combine with shallots and grated cheese. Season with cayenne, salt and white pepper to taste. Add chives and mix well. Pour into the tart shell and bake 25 minutes.

CELERY OIL: Peel the strings from the celery stalks and cut into 2 cm (3/4 in) lengths. Bring water and salt to a boil. Add celery and cook 3 minutes. Remove with a slotted spoon and plunge immediately into ice water. Drain and place in a food processor. With the motor running, add the walnut oil in a thin stream to make a thick sauce. Season with white pepper.

BELL PEPPER PESTO: Preheat the oven to 200C (400F). Cut off the stalk and rub the pepper with oil and salt. Bake 10 minutes until the skin blisters. Plunge into ice water. Peel, remove seeds and ribs and cut into chunks. Place in a food processor with the blanched garlic. With the motor running, add the oil in a thin stream until thick and creamy. Season with salt and white pepper and stir in the pine nuts.

GOAT CHEESE CREAM: Process the Snøfrisk and cottage cheese in a food processor until smooth. Add chives and season with salt and pepper.

TO SERVE: Cut the tart into wedges and place on individual plates. Top with goat cheese cream and garnish with the other ingredients as illustrated.

Cod and Ocean Crayfish Pizza
– 4 servings –

CRUSTS:
1 dl (scant 1/2 cup) olive oil
salt
1 dl (scant 1/2 cup) water
20 g (3/4 oz) fresh yeast
4 dl (1 2/3 cups) all-purpose flour

FILLING:
400 g (14 oz) boneless but not skinless cod fillets
salt and freshly ground white pepper
3 tablespoons olive oil

8 ocean crayfish
1/4 teaspoon sweet paprika
salt and freshly ground white pepper
3 tablespoons olive oil

OLIVE PUREE:
100 g (4 oz, approximately 1 3/4 dl, 3/4 cup) black olives, pitted
4 anchovy fillets
1 tablespoon capers
1 garlic clove, blanched 5 minutes
1/2 dl (3 tablespoons) olive oil
salt and freshly ground white pepper

SPINACH AND PARMESAN CREAM:
1 garlic clove, sliced
1 dl (scant 1/2 cup) extra virgin olive oil
100 g (4 oz) fresh spinach leaves, rinsed and dried
pinch salt
20 g (3/4 oz, about 3 tablespoons) grated Parmesan cheese
freshly ground white pepper

CRUSTS: Combine oil, salt, water and yeast well. Gradually add flour. Knead until smooth and elastic. Cover and let rest in a warm place about 30 minutes.

FILLING: Season the cod with salt and pepper and sauté in hot olive oil until just done, about 5 minutes. Season the ocean crayfish with sweet paprika, salt and pepper and sauté in hot oil, back side down, until cooked to medium.

OLIVE PUREE: Place olives, anchovies, capers and the cooked garlic clove in a food processor. With the motor running, add the olive oil in a thin stream to make a thick cream. Season with salt and white pepper.

SPINACH AND PARMESAN CREAM: Sauté garlic in olive oil. Remove the stalks and clean the spinach leaves well. Add to the pan with a little salt. Sauté until it wilts. Place in a food processor, add the Parmesan, and process to a smooth cream. Season with salt and white pepper.

TO ASSEMBLE: Preheat the oven to 220C (425F). Roll out the dough into eight 10 cm (4 in) circles. Pinch to form an edge. If possible, place a 9 cm (3 1/2 in) steel ring in the center of each. Fill with dried peas or rice, so the centers don't rise. Place on greased baking sheets and bake 20 minutes. Place a layer of spinach-Parmesan cream in the middle of each crust. Poach 3/4 the fish in salted water until it flakes, around 8 minutes. Drain and arrange the flakes in a tight circle over the spinach cream. Sauté the ocean crayfish and place on the fish. Sauté remaining fish, cut into strips and arrange on top. Garnish with a spoonful of olive puree and a chervil sprig.

POLLACK AND POTATOES LAYERED WITH ONION MARMALADE

- 4 SERVINGS -

600 g (1 2/3 lbs) boneless and skinless pollack fillets
salt and freshly ground white pepper
1 tablespoon butter
3 tablespoons olive oil

CRISPY POTATO LAYERS:
300 g (10 oz) almond (or other waxy) potatoes
1/2 teaspoon salt
2 tablespoons chopped chives
2 tablespoons melted butter

POTATO PUREE:
200 g (2 medium) potatoes
4 tablespoons (1/4 cup) whipping cream
1 garlic clove, minced
2 tablespoons butter
2 tablespoons chopped chives
salt and freshly ground white pepper

ONION MARMALADE:
8 shallots, peeled and halved
1 dl (scant 1/2 cup) Noilly Prat (or dry white wine)
2 dl (7/8 cup) light veal stock
1 tablespoon butter
salt and freshly ground white pepper

BACON-VINAIGRETTE:
50 g (3 tablespoons) butter
50 g (3 slices) bacon, diced
1 tablespoon sweet soy sauce (Indonesian ketjap manis)
1 tablespoon lime juice

Cut the fish into 8 pieces of equal size. Season with salt and white pepper. Heat butter and oil together. Fry fish until golden.

CRISPY POTATO LAYERS: Peel and shred potatoes. Dry thoroughly with paper towels, pressing out as much liquid as possible. Combine with salt, chives and butter. Heat a "krumkake" or pizelle iron (both available at specialty stores). Place a spoonful of potato mixture on the iron and cook until crispy. Make 12.

POTATO PUREE: Peel the potatoes and cook until tender in unsalted water. Steam until dry. Mash with cream, garlic, butter, chives, salt and freshly ground white pepper. Keep warm.

ONION MARMALADE: Combine shallots and Noilly Prat in a saucepan and cook until almost no liquid remains. Add stock and cook over high heat until about half the original amount remains. Pour into a food processor and process with the butter until smooth. Season with salt and pepper.

Bacon-vinaigrette: Melt the butter and skim off the clear liquid. Discard the milky liquid remaining in the bottom of the pan. Sauté the bacon in the clarified butter. Remove the pan from the heat and let the bacon rest 10 minutes. Combine with soy sauce and lime juice.

TO SERVE: Layer crispy potato sheets with fish, potato puree and onion marmalade in the center of four large plates. Drizzle bacon vinaigrette over. Garnish with fresh herbs, if desired.

Herbed Rack of Lamb with Marinated Eggplant
– 4 servings –

800 g (1 3/4 lbs) rack of lamb
salt and freshly ground white pepper
butter
8 sheets filo pastry
24 fresh basil leaves

Marinated eggplant:
1 eggplant
5 tablespoons (1/3 cup) olive oil
2 garlic cloves, finely chopped
1 shallot, finely chopped
1 dl (scant 1/2 cup) tomato concasse or thick tomato sauce
chopped fresh tarragon
chopped fresh basil
1 dl (1/3 cup) olive oil
salt and freshly ground white pepper

Eggplant confit:
2 eggplants
1/2 garlic clove, minced
2 tablespoons minced shallot
2 tablespoons butter
2 fresh rosemary leaves
1 teaspoon chopped fresh basil
salt and freshly ground white pepper

Baked bell peppers:
1 yellow bell pepper
1 red bell pepper
2 tablespoons olive oil
salt and freshly ground white pepper

Setubal jus:
2 dl (1 cup) red wine
2 dl (3/4 cup) setubal or sweet white wine such as Muscat de Baume de Venise
2 tablespoons minced shallots
1 tablespoon dried bolete (cepes) mushrooms
4 white peppercorns, crushed
8 dl (3 1/3 cups) lamb stock

Lamb: Bone the rack of lamb and remove all fat and membrane. There should be one long strip of boneless meat. Season with salt and freshly ground pepper and brown in butter. Pack in filo pastry covered with basil leaves. Reserve.

Marinated eggplant: Wash the eggplant and cut into 1 cm (1/2 in) slices. Grill over/under high heat. Reserve. Sauté garlic and shallot in olive oil until golden. Add tomatoes and cook to a thick sauce. Whisk in fresh herbs and oil. Season with salt and pepper. Brush the eggplant slices thoroughly with the marinade. Cover with plastic wrap and marinate about 1 hour. Heat thoroughly under the grill before serving.

Eggplant confit: Preheat the oven to 220C (425F). Wash the eggplants and halve lengthwise. Bake until they shrivel. Scrape out the pulp. Sauté garlic and shallot in butter until golden. Add remaining ingredients and cook until any liquid is evaporated. Season with salt and pepper. Transfer to a food processor and puree.

Baked bell peppers: Clean the peppers, removing the core, seeds and ribs. Rub with oil, salt and pepper. Bake about 15 minutes. Plunge immediately into ice water. Peel.

Setubal jus: Combine red wine and 1 1/2 dl (2/3 cup) and setubal with onion, mushrooms and seasoning. Reduce over high heat until about 1 dl (scant 1/2 cup) remains. Add lamb stock and reduce over high heat until about 4 dl (1 2/3 cups) remain. Just before serving, add remaining setubal and bring to a boil. Season with salt and pepper.

Preheat the oven to 220C (425F). Bake the pastry-covered lamb 5 minutes, then let rest 5-10 minutes before serving.

To serve: Arrange on hot plates as illustrated.

Semi-frozen Apple-Spice Cream with Candied Apricots
- 4 servings -

APPLE CREAM:
4 apples (preferably golden delicious)
1 dl (scant 1/2 cup) water
1 cinnamon stick
100 g (1 1/4 dl, 1/2 cup) sugar
1/2 dl (3 tablespoons) calvados
2 1/2 dl (1 cup) whipping cream

RASPBERRY-VANILLA SAUCE:
2 1/2 dl (1 cup) water
250 g (4 3/4 dl, 2 cups) raspberries
125 g (1 1/2 dl, 2/3 cup) sugar
1/2 vanilla bean

BASIL-CINNAMON SORBET:
1/2 dl (3 tablespoons) water
200 g (2 1/2 dl, 1 cup) sugar
1 cinnamon stick
1 bunch fresh basil
40 g (about 2 tablespoons) glucose
juice of 1/2 lemon

CRISPY LAYERS:
50 g (1/3 cup) flour
1 egg

CANDIED APRICOTS:
12 apricots
5 dl (2 cups) water
200 g (2 1/2 dl, 1 cup) sugar
pinch saffron
1/2 vanilla bean

CARAMEL CUPS:
125 g (4 oz, 1/2 cup) unsalted butter
125 g (1 1/2 dl, 2/3 cup) sugar
80 g (1 1/4 dl, 1/2 cup) flour
3-4 tablespoons half and half

SOUR CREAM TOPPING:
1/2 tablespoons dairy sour cream (do not use low fat sour cream)
1 1/2 tablespoons confectioner's sugar

100 g (4 oz, about 2 dl, 3/4 cup) raspberries

APPLE CREAM: Peel, core and cube the apples. Place in a saucepan with water, cinnamon and sugar and bring to a boil. Simmer until soft. Press through a sieve. Cool. Add calvados. Whip the cream and fold into the apple mixture. Divide among 4 individual serving rings/forms (about 7 cm, in diameter). Freeze.

RASPBERRY-VANILLA SAUCE: Bring water and berries to a boil. Mash berries and press through a sieve. Add sugar to the juice and bring to a simmer. Skim frequently, until the sauce is clear. Scrape the seeds from the vanilla bean and add. Reduce over high heat until syrupy.

BASIL-CINNAMON SORBET: Bring water, sugar and cinnamon to a boil. Remove from the heat and let steep about 2 hours. Sieve. When completely cool, pour into a food processor or use a vertical mixer. Add basil, glucose and lemon juice. Freeze in an ice cream maker or pour into a mold and freeze (then whirl in a food processor just before serving).

CRISPY LAYERS: Preheat the oven to 180C (350F). Combine ingredients. Make small tartlets in miniature muffin tins and bake until golden, about 8 minutes.

CANDIED APRICOTS:
Halve apricots and remove pits. Bring water, sugar, saffron and vanilla to a boil. Add apricots and simmer until the skin loosens. Remove and peel. Cool.

CARAMEL CUPS:
Preheat the oven to 180C (350F). Combine all ingredients until smooth. Spoon into circles on a parchment-covered baking sheet. Bake until golden, about 5 minutes. As soon as the cookies are removed from the oven, drape over tea cups to form bowls. Let cool.

SOUR CREAM TOPPING:
Whip sour cream with confectioner's sugar until stiff.

TO SERVE: Arrange as illustrated.

TRØNDELAG
– Trondheim 1000 years old, strawberries and cream...

It is 1000 years since Olav Trygvasson established Kaupangen (a market center) in Trondheim, the city on the river. There's a lot to see in such an old place, which is also the site of a cathedral and Norway's third largest city. What about a soccer match at Lekrendal? Rosenborg, the home team, have been Norwegian champions time after time. Or maybe a visit to Munkholmen? This beautiful island originally was a place of execution, but later it became a monastery, and from the end of the 1600's, a fort with thick walls. The cathedral, begun in 1152, is a must. And people come from far and wide to visit the collection of characteristic wooden houses from the 18th and 19th centuries plus the many old neighborhoods and farm complexes at the open-air museum.

Yes, the grid-shaped city with broad streets planned so carefully by General Cicignon in 1681 is well worth a visit. Especially now, in its jubilee year. Congratulations!

Gardens and – cream...

With its intensive gardening and agriculture, Trøndelag is something special. Also fish farming - salmon and trout mostly - is well developed. But it is mostly the Trønder berries we think of when we speak of "crops" in these parts. When berry season farther south in the country is over in August, the sweet, juicy berries from the districts around Trondheim fjord are ready to flood the country. And - they are best eaten on their own, topped with thick, Norwegian cream or sour cream. Cream and sour cream are important flavor and texture enhancers in Norwegian cooking. And it is the soul of Norwegian cream cakes. Yes, the quality of Norwegian dairy products couldn't be higher.

Milk has always held a special place. Everyone, small and large, drinks cold, fresh milk.

History

The history of Trøndelag goes further back than the 1000-year-old city of Trondheim. Norway's oldest assembly of the law, the Frostating, is here. Already in Viking times and in the Middle Ages, Frosta was the site of the lawmaking assembly and tribunal, the first form of government in our country.

Local delicacies are sodd (a kind of soup), skjenning, kaffebrød, and lefse (all baked goods). Both fishing along the coast and in the best salmon rivers attract people to Trøndelag. And the salmon appears in countless forms - poached, smoked, grilled, pickled, marinated and...fried in butter.

Name:
   Lars Lian
DOB:
   December 15, 1963
Present Position:
   Master pastry chef (partner), E. Erichsens Konditori, Trondheim.
Previous Positions:
   Pastry chef: Cip Cafe and Konditori, and Royal Garden Hotell, both Trondheim. Intern pastry chef at a number of well-known pastry shops in Denmark. Master pastry chef, Conten Cafe & Konditori, Oslo.
   Intern: L. Heine Cafe and Conditori, Vienna and a number of other places in Austria and Switzerland. Master pastry chef, Britannia Hotell, Trondheim.
Awards:
   Gold medal in Norwegian pastry chef contest 1990; Gold medal for best work with chocolate - Tema 91, Copenhagen; Gold - Best international exhibitor in Nordic, Herning, Denmark; Gold - Team competition 1990. Gold - Best national exhibitor and Gold - Best international exhibitor - Tema 93, Copenhagen. Gold - Nordic team championships, Oslo, 1995. Participated at World Championships for pastry chefs twice. In addition, a number of gold and silver medals with the Norwegian Culinary Team 1990/92 and 1992/96 American Culinary Classic; Salon Culinaire, Singapore; Culinary Olympics, Ika Hoga.

LARS LIAN
– World class pastry chef

Around 1990, Norway realized that it had fostered a pastry chef
of the same caliber as the middle-European masters. Lars Lian's name was always appearing in the newspapers.
This young man from Trondheim has his share of glittering medals from competitions.
Most of the time, though, he is a partner at Erichsen's Konditori in Trondheim.

Your philosophy, Lars Lian?

The most important thing is that good food should be real - and accessible to everyone.

What about Norwegian ingredients?

We are blessed with wonderful dairy products, invaluable in cooking and in baking. Butter, cream, creme fraiche - everything has a natural, true flavor.
Otherwise, berries, especially strawberries from Trøndelag, are tops. Norwegian fish and our flavorful lamb are also world class.

What do you like to eat best?

That depends upon the mood and the season. But freshly cooked crabs on an early autumn evening or a classic cod dinner in late winter are clear favorites. In addition, I like almost all Italian food and Tex-Mex dishes. There are a lot of favorites around here.

What about your style?

For the most part, it can be called modern pastry artistry, with a solid foundation in the central European pastry tradition, but "something" is always changing. I think it's called development.

Why did you choose to become a pastry chef?

Because it is a creative line of work. No two days are the same. You have to draw upon the best and most creative in yourself when a challenge comes along. It's unique work, really...

Is there time for other interests?

I have to admit that work and family take most of my time, and it's a lifestyle I enjoy. Otherwise, I like sports, especially soccer. And I don't say no to a fishing trip once in a while.

Do you ever have time to cook at home?

Sure, we make food at home. It's different and relaxing. I have to admit - we use a lot of garlic, olive oil, Parmesan cheese and good wine, when we really get down to it.

What is the most important thing for you?

On the job, it has to be to make desserts that guests never forget. In addition, I want to inspire my apprentices to be really competent and interested.

What about food in the future?

We should call attention to the Norwegian baking and cake traditions. Even though I don't deal with these on a daily basis, I think it would be a shame if good things like lefser, lumper and sveler (traditional soft flatbreads, the latter similar to a risen pancake) disappeared.
Also, we have to preserve our traditions, at least the best of them. I would like to draw attention to the possibilities we have with fish and game. It is this quality that future tourists should meet in their visit to Norway.

ERICHSEN'S NUT CAKE

*This cake has both nut and sponge cakes,
fruit filling (candied plums or pears, even cherries),
chocolate cream and chocolate flakes.*

NUT SPONGE BASE:
4-5 egg whites
1 tablespoon sugar
1 1/2 dl confectioner's sugar
160 g (4 3/4 dl, 2 cups) chopped hazelnuts or almonds

SPONGE BASE:
5 eggs
125 g (1 1/2 dl, 2/3 cup) sugar
125 g (2 dl, 3/4 cups) flour
grated zest of 1 lemon

CHOCOLATE CREAM:
125 g (4 1/2 oz) semi-sweet chocolate
1/2 dl (3 tablespoons) water
50 g (4 tablespoons, 1/4 cup) sugar
3 dl (1 1/4 cups) whipping cream

CHOCOLATE GARNISH:
200 g (7 oz) semi-sweet chocolate
2 tablespoons soybean oil

SUGAR SYRUP:
1 dl (1/3 cup) sugar
1 dl (1/3 cup) water
1-2 tablespoons kirsch, orange liqueur or cognac

7 dl (3 cups) fruit or berries
2 1/2 dl (1 cup) whipping cream
confectioner's sugar

NUT SPONGE BASE: Preheat the oven to 160C (325F). Line a 23 cm (9 in) springform pan with baking parchment. Beat egg whites and sugar to soft peaks. Combine confectioner's sugar and chopped nuts. Fold into the egg white mixture.
Pour into the prepared pan. Bake until golden, 30-40 minutes.

SPONGE BASE: Preheat the oven to 180C (350F). Grease and flour a 23 cm (9 in) springform pan. Beat eggs and sugar until light and lemon-colored. Sift the flour over the egg mixture and fold in lightly but thoroughly. Pour into the prepared pan. Bake about 35 minutes.

CHOCOLATE CREAM: Break the chocolate into small pieces and melt in a double boiler or in a microwave. Bring water and sugar to a boil. Add melted chocolate. Cool to lukewarm. Whip the cream and fold it into the chocolate mixture.

GARNISH: Break the chocolate into small pieces and melt in a double boiler or microwave. Whisk in the oil in a thin stream. Pour onto a large flat dish and cool to room temperature. Scrape flakes/shreds of chocolate with the back of a long knife.

SUGAR SYRUP: Combine sugar and water in a saucepan and bring to a boil. Simmer 1 minute. Remove from the heat and stir in your choice of flavoring.

Arrange your choice of fruit or berries on the nut sponge base. Spread with chocolate cream and build up to a hemispherical mound. Cut a 1 cm (1/2 in) layer of the sponge base and place over the chocolate cream. Sprinkle with flavored sugar syrup. Whip the cream and spread over the cake. Decorate with the chocolate flakes. Just before serving, sift confectioner's sugar over the cake.

Cappuccino Ice Cream Cake

*This is a wonderful dessert for special occasions.
It can be served on its own, but it's also good
with fresh strawberries or a citrus salad. The cake is built up
of layers of vanilla ice cream (parfait) and almond meringue sprinkled with espresso.*

ALMOND MERINGUE BASES:
*4 egg whites (from extra large eggs)
150 g (1 3/4 dl, 3/4 cup) sugar
90 g (1 1/2 dl, 2/3 cup) blanched almonds
cinnamon
cocoa*

VANILLA ICE CREAM (PARFAIT):
*6 egg yolks
scant 1 1/2 dl (2/3 cup, 120 g) sugar
scraped grains from 1 split vanilla bean
4 1/2 dl (2 cups) half and half
1 1/4 dl (1/2 cup) whipping cream*

ESPRESSO SYRUP:
*100 g (1 1/4 dl, 1/2 cup) sugar
1 dl (scant 1/2 cup) water
3/4 dl (1/3 cup) espresso (or 2 teaspoons instant coffee and 3/4 dl water)*

ALMOND MERINGUE BASES: Preheat the oven to 170C (350F). Line 2 baking sheets with parchment paper. Grind blanched almonds. Beat egg whites with half the sugar to soft peaks. Combine remaining sugar with the ground nuts and fold into the meringue. Spoon into a pastry bag and pipe 3 circles about 20 cm (8 in) in diameter. Sift a little cinnamon and cocoa on the meringues. Bake until light golden, about 25 minutes.

VANILLA ICE CREAM: Combine all ingredients with the exception of the cream in a saucepan and heat almost to boiling, whisking constantly. Remove from the heat as soon as the mixture starts to bubble (otherwise the eggs will "scramble") and continue whisking until the mixture has deflated slightly. Cool completely. Whip the cream and fold into the egg yolk mixture. Freeze in an ice cream machine or pour into a mold. Freeze. After about 30 minutes, remove the mold and stir. Refreeze.

ESPRESSO SYRUP: Combine sugar and water in a saucepan and bring to a boil. Add coffee and stir well. Cool.

Place one almond meringue base in a 23 cm (9 in) springform pan. Sprinkle until almost soaked with espresso syrup. Top with half the ice cream, then a new base. Repeat with syrup and remaining ice cream Top with remaining almond base. Freeze overnight. If storing for a longer time, wrap in plastic.

TO SERVE: Remove from the pan. Sift cocoa over the cake.

STRAWBERRY CAKE

ALMOND SPONGE BASE:
3 eggs
75 g (scant 1 dl, 3/8 cup) sugar
grated zest from 1/2 lemon (optional)
75 g (1 1/4 dl, 1/2 cup) flour
60 g (about 1 1/2 dl, 2/3 cups) coarsely chopped blanched almonds

STRAWBERRY CREAM:
500 g (1 lb, about 3 cups) fresh strawberries, cleaned
1 dl (scant 1/2 cup) water
100 g (1 1/4 dl) sugar
5-6 star anise
1 vanilla bean
2 passion fruit
3 dl (1 1/4 cups) whipping cream
7 sheets (4 teaspoons) unflavored gelatin

3/4 dl (1/3 cup) freshly squeezed orange juice (optional)

Preheat the oven to 180C (350F). Line a 23 cm (9 in) pan with baking parchment. Beat eggs and sugar until light and lemon-colored. Add lemon zest. Sift the flour over the egg mixture and fold in lightly but thoroughly. Fold in the chopped nuts. Bake about 35 minutes.

STRAWBERRY CREAM: Remove about 200 g (7 oz, 1 1/4 cups) pretty berries for garnish. Combine water, sugar, star anise, juice and peel from the passion fruit in a saucepan. Bring to a boil. Cool, then add remaining strawberries. Marinate at least 4-5 hours, preferably overnight in the refrigerator. Remove passion fruit shells, star anise and vanilla bean from the strawberry mixture and discard. Pour strawberry mixture into a food processor and puree. Soak the gelatin sheets in cold water (sprinkle the powdered gelatin over 3 tablespoons of the strawberry puree) to soften, about 5 minutes. Squeeze excess water from the gelatin sheets (disregard for powdered gelatin) and melt the gelatin in 1 dl (1/2 cup) of the strawberry puree. Stir into remaining puree, mixing well. Whip the cream and fold into the marinade.

Place the sponge base in the bottom of a 23 cm (9 in) pan. Halve the berries lengthwise and place around the sides. Sprinkle with orange juice, if desired. Pour the strawberry cream over the base and refrigerate overnight.

TO SERVE: Remove the cake from the pan. Decorate with grated white or milk chocolate and if desired, a layer of transparent red gelatin.

FRUITCAKE

LIGHT SPONGE BASE:
   2 eggs
   1 egg yolk
   60 g (3/4 dl, 1/3 cup) sugar
   30 g (3 1/2 tablespoons) flour
   2 tablespoons potato starch
   cinnamon

VANILLA CREAM:
   1 vanilla bean
   4 dl (1 2/3 cups) milk
   1 1/2 dl (2/3 cups) whipping cream
   100 g (1 1/4 dl, 1/2 cup) sugar
   35 g (4 tablespoons, 1/4 cup) cornstarch
   1/2 dl (3 1/2 tablespoons) milk
   1/2 dl (3 1/2 tablespoons) whipping cream

   plain cookie crumbs
   fresh raspberries

GELATIN TOPPING:
   2 1/2 dl (1 cup) water
   50 g (4 tablespoons, 1/4 cup) water
   4 sheets (2 teaspoons) unflavored gelatin
   vanilla, lemon zest (optional)

Preheat the oven to 230C (450F). Line a baking sheet with parchment paper and trace two 23 cm (9 in) circles on the paper. Beat eggs, egg yolk and sugar until thick and lemon-colored. Sift flour and potato starch over the egg mixture and fold in gently but thoroughly. Spoon the mixture within the traced circles. Carefully sift a little cinnamon over, then bake 6-7 minutes.

VANILLA CREAM: Split the vanilla bean lengthwise and scrape out all the grains. Place bean and grains in a saucepan with the milk, cream and sugar. Bring to a boil. Whisk cornstarch with the egg yolks, cream and milk until dissolved. Pour over the hot milk, whisking constantly. Return to the pan and return to a boil.

Place one base in the bottom of a 23 cm (9 in) springform pan. Pour in half the boiling vanilla cream. Make sure the cream goes all the way out to the edge. Top with the remaining base and pour over the remaining vanilla cream. Sprinkle with a thin layer of crumbs (to help the berries adhere to the cream better). Cover with fresh raspberries.

GELATIN TOPPING: Soak the gelatin sheets (sprinkle the powdered gelatin over 2 tablespoons of the) cold water to soften, about 10 minutes. While the gelatin is soaking, bring (remaining) water and sugar to a boil, then remove from the heat. Squeeze out excess water (disregard for powdered gelatin) and melt the gelatin in the hot sugar-water. Add vanilla or lemon zest, if desired. Simmer a few minutes. Cool until syrupy, then spoon a thin layer over the raspberries. Refrigerate until serving time. It is also possible to use fruit juice instead of water and to flavor with dessert wine or liqueur.

TIP: For an extra special effect, melt chocolate and brush it on a band of thick plastic (which fits around the cake). Wrap around the cake, plastic side out. Remove the plastic band when the cake is thoroughly chilled. Then there will be a "chocolate ring" around the cake.

TO SERVE: Serve with homemade spice ice cream or fruit sorbet.

ALMOND MACAROON CAKE

In 1862, a Belgian pastry chef's apprentice came to Erichsen's Pastry Shop in Trondheim, where he introduced a Belgian specialty, an almond macaroon cake. This new treat was called "fyrstekake." Today, it is a well-known Norwegian specialty. At Erichsen's, it is still the most noble of cakes. And T rondheimers in all parts of the country order it for Christmas. The bakery still uses the recipe from 1862, and it's our secret. We want to keep the original recipe for ourselves at Erichsen's. Anyway, it's too complicated to prepare in a home kitchen. Here is a simpler version, which anyone can make.

SWEET PASTRY:
3 dl (1 1/3 cups) flour
6 tablespoons butter
3/4 dl (1/3 cup) confectioner's sugar
1-2 egg yolks
3-5 tablespoons water

FILLING:
about 2 3/4 dl (1 1/4 cups) blanched almonds
2 dl (3/4 cup) sugar
1 tablespoon butter
2 egg yolks

SWEET PASTRY: Combine all ingredients to make a smooth dough. Wrap in plastic and refrigerate 1 hour. Preheat the oven to 170C (350F). Roll out 2/3 of the dough to fit a 22 cm (9 in) pie pan. Spread almond filling over the crust, pressing it evenly over the entire bottom. Roll out remaining dough, cut into strips and arrange in a lattice pattern over the filling. Bake on the lowest oven rack until light and firm, 45-60 minutes. Do not overbake. The cake should be a little soft inside.

Begin with the filling: Place the almonds in a bowl and add water to cover. Let rest overnight. Drain, then place in a food processor with the sugar and process until finely ground. Beat in butter and egg yolk.

Passion Fruit Mousse with Cocoa Sorbet and Licorice Caramel Sauce

ALMOND SPONGE BASE:
100 g (3 oz, 3/8 cup) unsalted butter
1 1/4 dl (1/2 cup) sugar
1 1/2 dl (2/3 cup) almonds
2 eggs
4 tablespoons (1/4 cup) flour

PASSION FRUIT MOUSSE:
3 sheets (1 1/2 teaspoons) unflavored gelatin
about 1 dl (scant 1/2 cup) passion fruit juice
3/4 dl (1/3 cup) sugar
juice of 1 orange
2 dl (3/4 cup) whipping cream

COCOA SORBET:
3 1/2 dl (1 1/2 cups) water
1 1/2 dl (2/3 cup) milk
1 3/4 dl (3/4 cup) sugar
40 g (1 1/4 oz) glucose
3/4 dl (1/3 cup) cocoa
100 g (3 1/2 oz) semi-sweet chocolate, chopped

ANISE SYRUP:
2 1/2 dl (1 cup) water
1 1/2 dl (2/3 cup) sugar
1 licorice root (about 50 g, 1 3/4 oz) or 6-8 whole star anise

ALMOND SPONGE BASE: Preheat the oven to 190C (375F). Line a 22 cm (9 in) springform pan with baking parchment. Place all ingredients in a food processor and puree until smooth. Pour into the prepared pan and bake 15-20 minutes.

PASSION FRUIT MOUSSE: Soak the gelatin sheets cold water (sprinkle the powdered gelatin over 2 tablespoons of the passion fruit juice) to soften, about 10 minutes. In a saucepan, bring (remaining) passion fruit juice to a boil and remove from the heat. Add sugar and stir until dissolved. Add orange juice. Squeeze out excess water (disregard for powdered gelatin) and dissolve the gelatin in the hot juice. Cool to room temperature. Whip the cream and fold into the juice mixture. Pour over the almond sponge base. Refrigerate overnight.

COCOA SORBET: Whisk all ingredients together in a saucepan. Simmer over low heat about 10 minutes. Stir chopped chocolate into the cocoa mixture. Cool completely, then puree in a food processor or use an immersion blender. Freeze in an ice cream machine.

LICORICE SYRUP: Crush the licorice stick. Bring sugar and water to a boil. Add licorice (star anise) and simmer until dissolved. Cool. If using star anise, strain before serving.

TO SERVE: Serve the cake on large plates with sorbet and syrup alongside. Garnish with fresh fruit and/or berries.

Almond Ring Cake

400 g almonds
360 g sifted confectioner's sugar
(sift first, then measure)
160 g sugar
4 egg whites

Blance 200 g of the almonds and let them dry. All the almonds shal be finely grounded. Combine almonds with the confectioner's sugar and the sugar in a large saucepan. Add the unbeaten egg whites and mix to a firm dough. Place the pan over low heat and knead until the dough get so hot that it is almost impossible to handle. Put the pan aside with a lit on.

Preheat the ovnen to 180°C.
Brush the ring pans with melted butter and have some semolina on. Spoon the dough into a cookie press or pastry tube with wide round tip. Press the dough into the rings, pressing the ends together to look as seamless as possible. Bake 8–10 minutes, until dry and firm outside, but still slightly soft inside. Cool slightly, then remove from the pans and cool completely.

For the icing, sift som confectioner's sugar (2 dl) and combine with egg white (1 egg white) to make a tick icing. Make a small cone of paper and cut off the tip. Pipe on garlands of icing and stack. Dekorate with flags, bonbons, candy or fresh strawberries (with chocolate).

FJORD NORWAY
– fish farming and coastal culture

Now we are in the center of that part of Norway which so many tourists have experienced. Just about everyone in the whole world knows about "The Fjords." This is where Germans, Japanese and Americans all are entranced by the sight of the wild mountains, waterfalls, unbelievably steep roads and small farms which cling to the edges of cliffs.

Fish is king here. Cod and salmon, halibut and pollack, all are brought in from the bountiful sea. But on land, they compete with sheep and goats which graze in steep grassy meadows. Salmon fishermen stand in chest-high waders in rushing rivers to fish wild salmon. The catch isn't always as great as one might want, but the excitement is still there for the sports fisherman.

TREES HEAVY WITH FRUIT

Norway's best fruit orchards are also in the fjord district. And we produce a significant crop of apples and cherries. The first fruit trees were brought to the Hardanger fjord by Cistercian monks in the 13th century. Flowering fruit trees in the meadows along the fjords are a sight to behold, and many travel far to experience all this beauty.

Here are great contrasts in nature - from rugged mountains to fertile fields, with the fjord as an important traffic artery. In these parts, the tourist tradition is more than 150 years old. In fjord country, wherever the ferry docked, people settled.

Folks from other parts of Norway often feel that those from Hardanger, Møre and Romsdal are a fascinating group. People from this rough and barren landscape always have had to depend upon their own inventiveness, resourcefulness and optimism to survive.

In fjord country and along the west coast, fish, naturally enough, have always been the most important food on the table. Grain was considered so precious that it was called "a loan from God." Even the early Frostatingslov (a medieval law document) stressed the importance of herring and other fish. It is written there that, "both on Sunday and on all other days, herring can be caught, if God guides them toward land." And fish became the most important commodity - even the Vikings traded dried fish for grain.

The many goats in this part of the country give vast quantities of milk for the dairy industry. This is big goat, small cow territory. Snøfrisk (goat cream cheese) and the ever popular sweet brown goat cheese is produced here.

Fish farming

Fish farming began here in the beginning of the 1960's. Most Norwegian salmon and trout come from farms along the coast. Nature has provided Norway with excellent conditions for fish farming - plentiful clean water, untouched, and to a degree, secluded nature and last, but not least, favorable water temperature, thanks to the gulf stream. Production of farmed fish has increased quickly. Norwegian salmon is now exported all over the world and is known for its high quality.
Cod, mussels and other mollusks are also farmed. Halibut is farmed on a small scale and could well be the farmed fish of the future. Farming of flat fish and lobster are still in the experimental stages.

Name:
Frank Bodo Baer
DOB:
October 16, 1963
Present Position:
Chef/consultant, The Norwegian Culinary Institute, Stavanger.
Previous Positions:
Chef de partie: Alta Hotell, Tree Kokker, Restaurant Bagatelle; Souschef/chef: Restaurant Bagatelle, Oslo; Refsnes Gods, Moss; Restaurant Holbergs Årstidene, Oslo. Administrative chef and product developer for planning and menus for the Olympic Games at Lillehammer, 1994; Administrative chef, Rica Holmenkollen Park Hotel, Oslo.
Awards:
Best man award at chef's school, Norwegian Hotel and Catering College. Norwegian champion in oyster opening 1987. Gold medal, Nordic team championship 1989/95. A number of gold and silver medals with the Norwegian Culinary Team 1988/92 and 1992/96 American Culinary Classic; Salon Culinaire, Singapore; and Culinary Olympics, Ika Hoga.

FRANK BAER
– From the Lillehammer Olympics to the Culinary Institute

Frank Baer was the administrative chef and product developer for planning and menus for the Winter Olympics at Lillehammer in 1994. Everyone talked about how successful the food was – too... Now he is chef/consultant at the Culinary Institute in Stavanger and partner at Markveien Mat & Vinhus, a super restaurant in Oslo.

Tell us a little about your food philosophy.

It's always changing, with age, values and according to my workplace. Choice and use of products is important, as well as how they are prepared. I set aside time to develop myself. Then I can use my knowledge and ability to improve and develop my food all the time. That way I can offer my guests good traditional food as well as newly developed dishes.

What about Norwegian products?

We have some top quality products, no doubt about it. Growing conditions this far north give them both distinctive flavor and a beautiful appearance.
But, it can be difficult to get exactly the product you want. Is it, for example, fair to pay the same price for all grades of lamb? The system should be such that if someone wants to pay more for top quality, it should be possible.
We also have some good dairy products. Snøfrisk (goat cream cheese) is an exciting new addition to the Norwegian cheese family. Goat milk cheeses are a popular trend, even abroad, and they are used in food preparation. Snøfrisk should have good potential on the export market.

What is your favorite dish?

There it comes again, the question every journalist asks. For me, it changes according to time, place and mood. One day I like a good hamburger, the next I visit a 3-star restaurant. I enjoy both. When I'm home alone with my daughter, I like to open a can of Joika (reindeer meatballs). My wife never serves that, so when she's out, we can enjoy this "forbidden delicacy."

What about your own style in the kitchen?

It's Norwegian and uncomplicated, but with exciting combinations, often using untraditional seasonings. Food should never be camouflaged – good ingredients should taste of what they are.

Why did you become a chef?

It was natural for me. I practically grew up at my father's restaurant in the west country. And when my brother Jarle (also a well-known Norwegian chef) chose this profession, I, too, wanted to follow in the same line of work. We are a real "family of chefs."
I also wanted to preserve the traditions of my father's place and our identity with Norwegian food.

Do you have time for other interests?

Not much, really. My family is the most important thing in my life and deserves my time and concern. Otherwise I am interested in wine. If I have any time left, I go over to Markveien Mat & Vinhus (which the brothers own together).

What do you think the future holds in store?

We have a dream of owning a hotel-restaurant, where I can stir the pots and where my wife Cecilie can run the hotel.
Otherwise I want to support my brother Jarle in every way, so that our restaurant can continue to maintain the standards it does today.

SALMON BURGERS WITH SMOKED JARLSBERG

– 4 SERVINGS –

BUNS:
(Makes 20)
100 g (3 1/2 oz, scant 1/2 cup) butter
3 1/2 dl (1 1/2 cups) milk
50 g (1 3/4 oz) fresh yeast
1 teaspoon salt
1/2 teaspoon baking powder
500 g (about 8 1/4 dl, 3 1/2 cups) flour
beaten egg
sesame seeds

BURGERS:
600 g (1 1/3 lbs) boneless and skinless salmon fillet
2 1/2 teaspoons salt
2 tablespoons potato starch (or cornstarch)
1/4 teaspoon white pepper
2 teaspoons minced parsley
2 teaspoons chopped chives
1 tablespoon minced onion
1 1/4 dl (1/2 cup) whipping cream
butter

MARINATED TOMATOES:
400 g (14 oz, 4 small) plum tomatoes
1 dl (scant 1/2 cup) olive oil
1/2 teaspoon salt
2 teaspoons tomato paste
1 teaspoon chopped fresh thyme
2 teaspoons balsamic vinegar (or red wine vinegar)
1/2 garlic clove, peeled
pinch white pepper

chopped pickle
chopped onion
8 slices smoked Jarlsberg cheese
lettuce

BUNS: Melt butter and add milk. Crumble in the yeast. Add salt, baking powder and enough flour to make a firm dough. Knead well. Place in a bowl, cover and let rise in a warm place until doubled. Knead again well and roll into 20 balls. Place on a greased baking sheet and let rise about 20 minutes. Preheat the oven to 200C (400F). Brush the buns with beaten egg and sprinkle with sesame seeds. Bake about 20 minutes.

BURGERS: Cube the fish and place in a food processor. Pulse until coarsely chopped (or cut by hand into 1/2 cm (1/4 in) dice). Add salt, starch, pepper, herbs and onion. Pour in the cream and pulse until the mixture just holds together. Form into 8 burgers. Fry in butter to desired doneness (they can be medium).

MARINATED TOMATOES: Cut an "x" at the stem end of each tomato. Dip in boiling water about 30 seconds. Transfer immediately with a slotted spoon to ice water. Peel and cut into wedges. Remove seeds with a spoon. Place remaining ingredients (not the tomatoes) in a food processor and puree. Pour over the tomatoes. Marinate at least 3 hours.

TO SERVE: Cut eight buns in half. Place a burger on each and top with chopped pickle, onion and a slice of smoked Jarlsberg. Place under the broiler until the cheese melts. Cover with bun tops. Serve with lettuce and marinated tomatoes. Serve with fried potatoes, if desired.

Salmon with Herb Risotto
- 4 servings -

Fish:
600 g (1 1/3 lbs) boneless and skinless salmon fillet
salt
water
olive oil

Sesame sheets:
2 egg whites
3 1/2 tablespoons soft butter
pinch salt
pinch sugar
scant 1 dl (1/3 cup) flour
butter
3 tablespoons mixed black and white sesame seeds

Herb risotto:
2 tablespoons minced shallot
2 tablespoons olive oil
about 2 dl (7/8 cup) arborio rice
6 1/2 dl (2 3/4 cups) fish stock
1 teaspoon salt
freshly ground white pepper
2 tablespoons chopped chives
2 tablespoons minced parsley
2 tablespoons chopped fresh chervil
150 g (5 oz, about 3 dl, 1 1/4 cups) freshly grated Parmesan cheese
2 tablespoons butter

Saffron sauce:
2 teaspoons water
1/2 teaspoon saffron
3 shallots, minced
2 tablespoons unsalted butter
1 dl (1/3 cup) white wine
200 g (7 oz) cold unsalted butter, diced
salt and pepper

Spinach:
200 g (8 oz) fresh spinach
butter
1/4 teaspoon sugar
salt and pepper

Fish: Cut the fish into pieces of equal size. Make a brine of salt and water and add the fish. Let soak about 2 hours. Preheat the oven to 60C (140F). Drain the fish and place in a large oven proof dish. Pour olive oil over the fish to cover. "Cook" the fish in the oven to desired doneness - it can be served "medium." Remove fish from the oil and drain.

Sesame sheets: Preheat the oven to 210C (400F). Beat egg whites and butter. Add salt and sugar. Gradually add flour. Let rest 30 minutes. Grease a cold baking sheet with butter. Spread the mixture over the sheet. Sprinkle with sesame seeds. Bake until golden, 6-8 minutes. Cool.

Herb risotto: Sauté shallots in oil about 2 minutes. Add rice and mix well with the oil. Add stock. Simmer over low heat, stirring constantly, until all liquid is absorbed by the rice. Season with salt and pepper. Just before serving, fold in the herbs, Parmesan cheese and butter. If the rice seems dry, add a little more fish stock.

Saffron sauce: Heat water and saffron and reserve. Sauté shallots in butter. Add wine and reduce until the consistency of marmalade. Beat in the cold butter over low heat to make a thick sauce. Season with salt, pepper and saffron-water.

Spinach: Remove the stalks and clean the leaves well. Melt the butter in a saucepan with the sugar, salt and pepper. Steam the spinach until it wilts. Stir with the garlic-fork.

To serve: Place sesame sheets, salmon and spinach in 2-3 layers on top of one another. Divide the risotto among four deep dishes and top with the salmon layers. Spoon saffron sauce all around. Garnish with parsley, if desired.

Marinated Salmon Sandwich

- 4 servings -

MARINATED SALMON:
1 kg (2 1/4 lbs) boneless and skinless salmon fillet
1 tablespoon coarsely crushed black pepper
4 teaspoons salt
3 tablespoons sugar
2 tablespoons cognac
2 tablespoons dry sherry
1 teaspoon dried dill
1 1/4 dl (1/2 cup) chopped dill

BREAD:
4 dl (1 2/3 cups) water
75 g (2 3/4 oz) fresh yeast
4 dl (1 2/3 cups) natural yogurt
4 teaspoons honey
4 tablespoons (1/4 cup) olive oil
2 teaspoons salt
2 dl (3/4 cup) whole wheat berries
2 dl (3/4 cup) sesame seeds
4 dl (1 1/2 cups) coarsely ground whole rye flour (from a health food store)
about 1 1/3 liters (5 1/2 cups) flour

MUSTARD SAUCE:
3 tablespoons sweet mustard (not hot dog mustard)
2 tablespoons whole grain mustard
1 tablespoon Dijon mustard
4 tablespoons (1/4 cup) sugar (or a little less)
2 dl (7/8 cup) corn oil
2 1/2 tablespoons olive oil
3 tablespoons cold water
4 teaspoons cider vinegar
pinch salt
pinch pepper
3 tablespoons chopped fresh dill

butter
fresh dill

MARINATED SALMON: Arrange the fish in a glass dish or in a plastic bag. Sprinkle with remaining ingredients. Cover with plastic or seal the bag. Marinate 3 days, turning the fish several times, so that it is always covered in marinade. Remove from the marinade and dry lightly. Cover with plastic wrap and refrigerate until serving time.

BREAD: Heat the water to body temperature. Crumble yeast in a large bowl. Add water and stir to dissolve. Add yogurt, honey, oil and salt. Add wheat berries, sesame seeds and the coarse flour. Knead in the remaining flour to make a stiff dough. Cover and let rise until doubled. Turn out onto a floured board and knead well. Form into a large round loaf and place on a greased baking sheet. Let rise about 20 minutes. Preheat the oven to 200C (400F). Bake about 45 minutes. Cool.

MUSTARD SAUCE: Combine the mustards and the sugar in a bowl. Whisk in the oil in a thin stream. Thin with cold water, if necessary. Stir in remaining ingredients.

TO SERVE: Halve bread horizontally. Hollow out the center in one piece. Cut the center into small slices and spread with butter. Thinly slice the salmon and place on half the bread slices. Top with the rest. Trim to make sandwiches of similar size. Stack in the hollow loaf. Serve with mustard sauce. Garnish with dill.

LIGHTLY SALTED AND SMOKED LEG OF LAMB
- 4 SERVINGS -

800 g (1 3/4 lbs) boned and trimmed lightly salted and smoked leg of lamb
water
1 bay leaf
1 teaspoon black peppercorns
1 sprig parsley
1/2 teaspoon dried thyme
1 garlic clove, crushed
1 onion, coarsely chopped

VEGETABLES:
100 g (4 oz, 1 medium) onion
100 g (4 oz, 1/4 medium) celeriac
100 g (4 oz, 2 small) carrots
100 g (4 oz, 3 small) parsley roots
100 g (4 oz, 1 medium) leek

SAUCE:
1 tablespoon butter
1-2 tablespoons flour
2 dl (1 cup) cooking liquid
1 dl (1/2 cup) whipping cream
1/2 dl (1/2 cup) milk
3 tablespoons creme fraiche or dairy sour cream (do not use low-fat)
salt and freshly ground white pepper
lemon juice
1 tablespoon chopped chives
2 tablespoons chopped parsley

POTATOES:
about 800 g (1 3/4 lbs) almond (or other waxy) potatoes
1 dl (1/3 cup) balsamic vinegar
salt and pepper
1 dl (1/3 cup) olive oil
1 dl (1/3 cup) vegetable oil
2 teaspoons chopped chives

Slice the lamb. Bring enough water just to cover the lamb to a boil. Add bay leaf, pepper, parsley, thyme, garlic and onion. Add the meat and simmer over low heat until tender. This is usually tender meat, so it doesn't take long. Cool the meat in the cooking liquid.

Before making the sauce, remove the meat and reduce the liquid over high heat to make the 2 dl (3/4 cup) needed for the sauce.

VEGETABLES: Clean and peel the vegetables. Cut into slices or batons. Cook separately in lightly salted water until tender.

SAUCE: Melt butter and stir in the flour. Whisk in the stock. Bring to a boil. Add cream and milk and simmer 15 minutes. Whisk in the creme fraiche, salt, pepper and lemon juice. Just before serving, add the chopped herbs. If using sour cream, do not allow the sauce to boil when reheating.

POTATOES: Scrub the potatoes well and boil in their skins. Remember that they should just simmer, not boil, or they will disintegrate. Whisk vinegar, salt and pepper and gradually add both kinds of oil. Peel and slice the potatoes (1/2 cm, 1/4 in thick). Lightly toss potatoes and dressing.

TO SERVE: Arrange potato slices in a circle along the outside edge of 4 dinner plates. Top with a slice of lamb and arrange the vegetables all around. Drizzle with a little sauce and serve the rest alongside. Garnish with fresh herbs.

Baked Halibut

- 4 servings -

Spice blend:
1 tablespoon coriander seeds
1 tablespoon powdered ginger
1 tablespoon peppercorns
2 star anise
1 tablespoon ground mace
1 teaspoon cinnamon
1 teaspoon cardamom seeds
2 tablespoons salt

Sauce:
2 dl (3/4 cup) concentrated lobster stock
1/2 dl (3 tablespoons) concentrated veal stock
50 g (3 tablespoons) cold butter
Pernod
lemon juice
1 teaspoon chopped chives
salt and pepper
2 teaspoons cornstarch stirred into 2 teaspoons cold water

Garnishes:
160 g (6 oz, 1 small tail) lobster meat
100 g (4 oz, 1 1/2 dl, 2/3 cup) dried tomatoes
olive oil
150 g (5 oz) fresh spinach leaves
1 garlic clove, chopped
butter
sugar, salt and pepper
200 g (8 oz, 1 small) zucchini

Celeriac timbales:
200 g (8 oz, 1/2 medium) celeriac
2 dl (3/4 cup) whipping cream
3 eggs
1/2 garlic clove, peeled
salt and pepper

Potatoes:
400 g (14 oz) almond (or other waxy) potatoes, in wedges
100 g (1/3 cup) clarified butter
100 g (4 oz) shiitake mushrooms
salt and pepper
1 tablespoon chopped chives

Deep-fried black salsify:
2 black salsify
oil

Fish:
1 1/4 kg (2 3/4 lbs) halibut (without fins) in one piece
clarified butter

Spice blend: Grind all the spices and mix in the salt.

Sauce: Bring lobster and veal stock to a boil. Reduce until it thickens slightly. Beat in cold butter in pats. Season with Pernod, lemon juice, chives salt and pepper. If desired, thicken with cornstarch stirred into cold water.

Garnishes: Sauté lobster and tomatoes in olive oil. Remove the stalks from the spinach and clean the leaves well. Melt the butter in a saucepan and sauté the spinach with the garlic until wilted. Season with sugar, salt and pepper. Combine. Cut the zucchini into thin strips and form into cylinders. Fill with lobster mixture.

Celeriac timbales: Peel and slice the celeriac. Boil until tender. Drain. Preheat the oven to 110C (220F). Place in a food processor with cream, eggs, garlic, salt and pepper and puree. Divide among 4 individual timbale forms and cook in a water bath until set, about 20 minutes.

Potatoes: Sauté in butter until tender. Remove the stems from the mushrooms and slice. Sauté until soft. Cool. Layer potatoes and mushrooms in a dish and place in the refrigerator. Heat in the oven with the fish the last 5-10 minutes. Cut into slices. Garnish with chopped chives.

Fish: Preheat the oven to 250C (450F). Brush the fish with clarified butter. Sprinkle generously with the spice blend. Bake until just done, 15-20 minutes, according to thickness. Brush with butter several times during the cooking process.

Deep-fried black salsify: Peel and thinly slice. Deep-fry in hot oil until golden.

To serve: Serve the fish whole with vegetables, sauce and garnishes as illustrated.

Bacalao Superiore

– 4 servings –

600 g dried salt cod
1 liter (quart) court bouillon (water with white wine, garlic, pepper and fresh herbs

Sauce:
100 g (4 oz, about 1 1/2 dl, 2/3 cup) minced shallots
50 g (2 oz, scant 1 dl, 1/3 cup) chopped dried tomatoes
1 teaspoon tomato paste
2 garlic cloves, minced
1 tablespoon chopped chile pepper (seeds and ribs removed)
1 can (400 g, 14 oz) chopped tomatoes
50 g (2 oz, scant 1 dl, 1/3 cup) pitted black olives, chopped
2 teaspoons chopped chives
1 teaspoon honey
salt and pepper

Basil oil:
2 dl (3/4 cup) olive oil
leaves from 1 large bunch basil
1/2 garlic clove, peeled
1 dl (1/3 cup) water
salt and pepper

Potatoes:
800 g (1 3/4 lbs) almond (or other waxy) potatoes
butter

fresh herbs
dried tomatoes

Soak the fish about 5 days, changing the water daily. On the day of serving, bring the court bouillon to a boil. Cut the fish into serving pieces and poach about 10 minutes in simmering bouillon.

Sauce: Sauté shallots, dried tomatoes, tomato paste, garlic and chile in oil. Add tomatoes, olives and chives. Season with honey, salt and pepper.

Basil oil: Combine all ingredients in a food processor and puree until smooth.

Potatoes: Peel the potatoes and cut into wedges. Fry in butter until golden brown. The potatoes can be finished off in the oven.

To serve: Divide fish and "sauce" among 4 deep dishes. Serve the potatoes alongside and drizzle basil oil over. Garnish with fresh herbs and dried tomatoes, if desired.

Warm Cherries with Red Wine Sauce and Cinnamon Ice Cream
- 6-8 servings -

Soup:
1 bottle Cote de Rhone
3 tablespoons red wine vinegar
2 dl (7/8 cup) sugar
1 tablespoon cornstarch dissolved in 1 tablespoon cold water
1 kg (2 1/4 lbs) pitted morello cherries
1 vanilla bean

Pastry rings:
8 sheets puff pastry
egg yolk
water

Cinnamon ice cream:
2 dl (7/8 cup) milk
1 1/2 teaspoons ground cinnamon
3 tablespoons sugar
1 dl (scant 1/2 cup) whipping cream
3 egg yolks

fresh lemon balm or mint

Sauce: Split the vanillabean, bring wine, vinegar and vanillabean to a boil. Reduce over high heat until half the original amount remains. Add sugar and cook until dissolved. Thicken with cornstarch. Pour over the cherries.

Pastry rings: Preheat the oven to 200C (400F). Defrost pastry sheets 15 minutes. Brush with egg yolk. Cut out circles with cutters of two different sizes and place on a parchment lined baking sheet. Bake 15-20 minutes.

Cinnamon ice cream: Heat milk, cinnamon and sugar, stirring until the sugar is dissolved. Whisk in cream and egg yolks. Cool, then freeze in an ice cream maker. Or pour into a mold and freeze. Remove the mold after about 30 minutes and stir well. Refreeze.

To serve: Drain the cherries, reserving the sauce. Remove the vanilla bean. Place pastry circles in the bottom of six to eight dessert bowls. Arrange the cherries on the pastry. Top with ice cream. Garnish with lemon balm or mint. Heat the sauce and serve alongside.

ROGALAND
- an abundance of most things

Rogaland, the southern part of Vestlandet, is like a flat kitchen garden in many places. Jæren (called Norway's breadbasket), with the most fertile soil in the country, provides fresh vegetables for the entire population. Potato and grain fields stretch out in a sea of gold alongside some of the most beautiful beaches on the North Sea. But it was no easy task for our forefathers, who had to remove rocks as big as houses, in order to make these kitchen gardens. The islands of Ryfylke produce greenhouse tomatoes and other "tropical fruits."

ROGALAMB

Sheep and lamb graze on peaceful fields of heather which extend inland from the sea. Rogalamb, also called star lamb from Jæren has a nice ring to the words, and more than 150,000 animals are slaughtered every year in this area. Norwegian lamb is among the finest meat in the world, finely muscled and always tender. In addition, it is juicy and has a mild but distinctive flavor. The animals roam freely every summer, grazing on fresh grass and herbs. Lamb and mutton have long- established traditions in the Norwegian kitchen and have been used in countless ways - fresh, salted, smoked, dried, singed, scalded and dried, just to name a few. Among other things, our ancestors used special "tricks" to keep lamb and other meat fresh. The meat was placed in sour milk (great-grandmother's vacuum packaging) and could stay fresh there for up to two weeks, even in the heat of summer.

WONDERFUL SEAFOOD

In these parts, people smile just thinking about a bag of fresh shrimp bought straight from the boat. Fresh fjord shrimp! They're best when you take the trouble to shell them yourself. When the shrimp boats dock with newly cooked shrimp, an entire catch gets sold in no time. And you also can find crab, mussels, ocean crayfish, lobsters, sea snails and scallops in Norway's oil city, Stavanger.

Crab season comes in late summer and early fall. Crab lovers go crabbing at dusk, and they cook their catches in saltwater.

A SEA TO SKIM

Eigersund in Rogaland is Norway's biggest fishing port, but all kinds of fish are processed in the plants along the coast. When Norwegians talk about shellfish, especially shrimp (a favorite all over the country) their thoughts frequently travel to these stretches of sea. Stavanger's great poet and author, Alexander Kielland, wrote this about the coastal people of Rogaland:
"They live their whole lives with faces turned towards the sea. The ocean is their company, their adviser, their friend and their enemy, their employer and their graveyard."

Large and small fish processing plants are spread along the coast. The establishment of these plants has been important for the development of the local economy in coastal districts. Many local, decentralized fishing docks and processing plants are important for coastal fishing fleets, which are unable to transport their catches over long distances.

Name:
Harald Osa

DOB:
May 10, 1958

Present Position:
Manager/superviser, The Norwegian Culinary Institute, Stavanger

Previous Positions:
Training periods at Hotel de France, Dodin Bouffant and at Gerard Pangaud, France.
Chef de Cuisine, Jans Mat & Vinhus in Stavanger.

Awards:
The Golden Chef's Hat 1986, Chef of the Year 1986.
A number of gold and silver medals with the Norwegian Culinary Team 1986/88, 1988/92, 1992/96 at the Culinary Olympics Ika Hoga; Salon Culinaire, Singapore; American Culinary Classic and others. Osa has published a number of cookbooks and appears on TV every week. The last few years, he has traveled around the world promoting Norwegian food and products.

HARALD OSA
- the boss himself...

Harald Osa is in charge of the Culinary Institute of Norway in Stavanger. The institute provides courses and consulting regarding all aspects of food, from recipes and product development to preparation and presentation. The Institute works with everyone in the food industry.

He combines this with professionalism at the highest level as well as enthusiasm. It is not just by chance that Osa is the leader of our national culinary team preparing for the Culinary Olympics in Berlin.

What are your thoughts regarding food?

I grew up by the moors near the sea at Jæren. I build on my culinary heritage and on the experience I have gained professionally. But the basis of my food philosophy is the demand for the absolute best ingredients and the inspiration these give.

What about Norwegian products?

Norway has the best conditions for excellent products, considering our location, the quality and amount of light and the long growing period. That encourages development of both flavor and appearance. Shellfish and fish, lamb, game, berries and vegetables are good examples. But we have to improve the way we handle and store these ingredients. We have to dare to demand the best from our producers and wholesalers and complain if the wares aren't good enough. That's the only way to do it.
Fortunately, we do have some flagships. Fish and game are first rate. When it comes to dairy products, I have to mention Jarlsberg cheese. USA imports more of it than any other cheese. It says a lot when this cheese sells better in the US than in Norway!

What is your favorite food?

That depends on the time and the occasion. My pleasure over a pot of steaming mussels on the beach or my mother's boiled beef and soup on a white damask tablecloth can be just as great and heartfelt as the experience of dining at one of the best restaurants in France.

What about your own personal style?

I strive to balance my French-inspired philosophy with Norwegian practicality and the best local ingredients. Respect for raw materials must be there at all times.

Why did you choose to become a chef?

Already as a child, I was inspired by two unknown food artists - my mother and her mother. Thanks to interesting and exciting experiences in their kitchens, I have chosen a career which has given me professional challenges, wonderful experiences, responsibility - and good friends.

Is there enough time in the day? What about other interests?

There just has to be. With two little charmers in the family, there's no problem of too much leisure time. The children and my wife Donna are my first priority. Otherwise, it takes quite a bit of time guiding the culinary team towards the Culinary Olympics in Berlin. We are aiming for medals of the glittering variety, and that demands hour upon hour, even day after day of patient practice.

What about food in your home kitchen?

It's mostly family-style food, food the children like. It's fantastic to come home and start cooking the evening meal with both of them beside me. They love it when they get to stir, taste and help out.

What is the most important thing to you?

Outside of my family? Concern for products and flavor. To be able to develop dishes with respect for the ingredients. To bring out the natural flavors. You have to want to stand in the kitchen, to use the time it takes to develop and create good things, things that are worth presenting to one's own pupils, suppliers and, most importantly, to one's guests.

What about food in the future?

My profession is international. Chefs have to learn from one another. There will be even more demands on our handiwork in the future, because food will be better and purer. But we also have to retain the best of the Norwegian kitchen and continue to progress, with an international outlook and high ambitions.

Lightly-salted cod and smoked shrimp with almond potato puree

– 4 SERVINGS –

400 g (14 oz) boneless and skinless lightly-salted cod fillets

POTATO PUREE:
300 g (10 oz) almond (or other waxy) potatoes
100 g (3 oz, 1/3 cup) butter
1 dl (1/3 cup) milk
salt and pepper

CRISPY POTATO SLICES:
2 almond (or other waxy small) potatoes
50 g (3 tablespoons) clarified butter
salt and pepper

SPINACH:
12 large fresh spinach leaves
1 tablespoon butter

TOMATO SAUCE:
3 large tomatoes
2 shallots
2 tablespoons butter
1 tablespoon chopped chives
salt and pepper

200 g (7 oz) shelled smoked shrimp

Bring enough unsalted water to just cover the fish to a boil. Add the cod, cover and remove from the heat. Remove when cooked through, about 8 minutes.

POTATO PUREE: Peel the potatoes and cook in unsalted water. Drain and steam until dry. Mash with butter and milk and season with salt and pepper.

CRISPY POTATO SLICES: Preheat the oven to 180C (350F). Scrub the potatoes well and thinly slice lengthwise. Dry well with a towel. Dip in clarified butter. (To clarify butter, melt, then spoon off the clear fat and discard the milky solids). Place the slices in one layer on a baking sheet. Bake until golden brown and crispy, 6-8 minutes. Drain on paper towels, then season with salt and pepper.

SPINACH: Remove the stalks and clean the leaves well. Melt the butter in a large saucepan and steam the spinach until it wilts.

TOMATO SAUCE: Cut an "x" at the stem end of each tomato. Dip in boiling water about 30 seconds. Transfer immediately with a slotted spoon to ice water. Peel, seed and dice. Peel and mince the shallots. Sauté shallots in butter until transparent. Add tomatoes and chives. Season with salt and pepper. Do not heat the sauce too much - it is supposed to be served lukewarm.

TO SERVE: Heat the potato puree. Fold in chunks of fish and the smoked shrimp. Divide the mixture among four deep dishes. Spoon tomato sauce all around. Arrange spinach and crispy potato slices on top.

BROCHETTES OF SALMON AND HALIBUT IN SOY SAUCE MARINADE
– 4 APPETIZER SERVINGS –

250 g (8 oz) boneless and skinless salmon fillet
250 g (8 oz) boneless and skinless halibut fillet

MARINADE/SAUCE:
2 shallots
2 garlic cloves
25 g (1 oz, 4x2x2 cm chunk, 1 1/2 in cube) fresh ginger (do not use dried, ground)
3/4 dl (1/3 cup) lemon juice
1/2 dl (3 tablespoons) dry white wine
1 dl (scant 1/2 cup) soy sauce
3/4 dl (1/3 cup) sugar
1/4 fresh red chile pepper
oil or butter
2 teaspoons cornstarch dissolved in 1 tablespoon water
2 tablespoons cold butter
2 tablespoons chopped chives

CREAMED SCALLIONS:
8-10 scallions
1 tablespoon butter
1 dl (scant 1/2 cup) creme fraiche or dairy sour cream (do not use low-fat)
salt and pepper

Cut salmon and halibut into 2 cm (3/4 in) cubes. Try to cut them so that everyone gets the same number of cubes.

MARINADE: Peel shallots, garlic and ginger. Cut into chunks. Place in a food processor with lemon juice, white wine, soy sauce and sugar. Puree until smooth. Pour into a plastic bag, add the fish cubes and marinate overnight in the refrigerator.

Remove the fish from the marinade, dry lightly and arrange alternately on sate sticks. Brown in oil or butter in a large pan over medium heat. They also can be grilled.

SAUCE: Strain the marinade into a saucepan. Bring to a boil. Thicken with cornstarch, if desired. Just before serving, beat in the butter in pats and fold in the chives.

CREAMED SCALLIONS: Wash, trim and thinly slice the scallions. Steam in butter over low heat. Season with salt and pepper. As soon as the scallions are soft, stir in the creme fraiche. Adjust seasonings, if necessary.

TO SERVE: Arrange the brochettes on four plates. Spoon creamed scallions and sauce alongside. Deep-fried potato sticks and fresh watercress are delicious with this dish, but you also could serve it just with bread rolls.

Shrimp in Their Shells with Herb Sauce and Toast

Count on 300 g (10 oz) shrimp in their shells per person

> Herb sauce for 4
> (easy to multiply):
> 1 1/2 dl (2/3 cup) mayonnaise
> 3 dl (1 1/4 cups) light sour cream
> 2 tablespoons lemon juice
> 2 tablespoons minced parsley
> 2 tablespoons chopped fresh tarragon
> 1 tablespoon chopped fresh chives
> 2 tablespoons chopped fresh basil
> salt and pepper
>
> Toast:
> fresh white bread
> butter

Shrimp: Use a bowl at least 10 cm (4 in) in diameter. Arrange the fresh shrimp overlapping (heads toward the middle) in rows to make one flat layer. Only the curves of the tails should be visible from the outside of the bowl. Repeat until the bowl is filled. Every third layer, press down well with a flat plate. (With the plate holding all the shrimp in place, turn the bowl upside down, to see how the arrangement will look when served.) When the bowl is full, press down with a flat plate one more time.
Place a serving platter over the bowl, then unmold carefully. You should have a beautiful shrimp centerpiece.
For an impressive centerpiece, you need at least 3 kg (6 1/2 lbs) of shrimp. If you plan a big party, you can make even make this one with 20 kg (45 lbs) of shrimp, `but then you need a 15 liter (quart) bucket!

Herb sauce: Combine all ingredients in a bowl with salt and pepper to taste.

Toast: Cut the bread into finger-thick slices. Sauté in butter until golden.

To serve: Place the shrimp centerpiece on the table. The guests shell the shrimp themselves. Serve herb sauce and toast alongside. Remember bowls for shrimp shells and finger bowls.

Sardines on Toast

There are all kinds of Norwegian sardines on the market, from traditional ones in oil to more modern ones in tomato, garlic and mustard sauces. The newest kind are "vintage" sardines, produced for the first time in 1994. They were caught in the Skånevik fjord and canned in Skånevik.

Sardine usage varies from country to country. In Norway, we eat them on a slice of bread. Sardines in the traditional manner are good as canapés with drinks.

Choose the sardines you like best. Arrange them on small pieces of white bread (cut into fancy shapes, if desired) which have been browned in butter. If using sardines in oil, be sure to drain them first. If the sardines are canned in a sauce, use some of the sauce as garnish.

Combine creme fraiche or sour cream (do not use low-fat sour cream - it doesn't pipe well) mixed with chopped fresh herbs. Spoon into a pastry tube and pipe rosettes of herb cream on the sardine toasts. Garnish with onion, mustard, tomato and cucumber wedges.

Herbed Lamb Filet with Aromatic Vegetables
- 4 servings -

about 3/4 kg (2 lbs) boneless lamb loin (untrimmed)
oil
3 tablespoons chopped fresh herbs (such as rosemary, parsley and thyme)
3 tablespoons butter
salt and pepper

Aromatic vegetables:
3 ripe beefsteak tomatoes
2 shallots
2 bay leaves
4 medium mealy potatoes
4 tablespoons (1/4 cup) butter
salt and pepper
1 onion
1 red bell pepper
1 small zucchini
1 garlic clove
150 g (5 oz) shiitake mushrooms

Thyme jus:
1 dl (1/3 cup) dry white wine
3 shallots, minced
5 dl (2 cups) concentrated lamb stock
2 tablespoons chopped fresh thyme
1 tablespoon cold butter (optional)

Basil oil:
1 small garlic clove
1/2 bunch parsley
1 dl (1/3 cup) extra virgin olive oil
1/2 bunch fresh basil

Deep fried celeriac:
about 150 g (5 oz) celeriac
oil
salt

Preheat the oven to 180C (350F). Trim fat as closely as possible without removing all of it. Remove back tendon. Tie with string to make a compact, even piece of meat. Rub with oil and chopped herbs. Brown in butter over low heat. Roast about 5 minutes. Season with salt and pepper. Let rest about 10 minutes. Just before serving, return to the oven for about 4 minutes. Slice, making sure everyone gets the same number of slices.

Aromatic vegetables: Cut an "x" at the stem end of each tomato. Dip in boiling water about 30 seconds. Transfer immediately with a slotted spoon to ice water. Peel, seed and chop. Peel and mince the shallots. Simmer tomato, shallots and bay leaves over low heat until the consistency of thick porridge. Peel and cube (1 cm, 1/2 in) the potatoes. Brown lightly in butter. Season with salt and pepper.
Clean/peel onion, bell pepper and squash and cut into small dice. Mince the garlic. Sauté vegetables in butter until transparent.
Remove stems from the mushrooms and cut each cap into 4-6 pieces. Sauté and season to taste.
Preheat the oven to 130C (275F).
Remove the bay leaves from the tomato sauce and combine with the other vegetables. Season, if necessary. Transfer to an oven proof dish (or individual dishes). Bake until potatoes are soft. This mixture tastes even better if it sits a while before serving.

Thyme jus: Combine white wine and shallot in a saucepan. Reduce over high heat until 1/3 of the original amount remains. Add stock and bring to a boil. Season with salt and pepper. Just before serving, add fresh thyme. Beat in the cold butter in pats, if desired.

Basil oil: Peel and chop the garlic. Chop the parsley. Cook in olive oil over low heat 2-3 minutes. Chop the basil and add. Puree in a food processor or use an immersion blender.

Deep-fried celeriac: Peel, clean and shred the celeriac. Heat the oil in a deep fryer to 160C (325F). Fry the shreds until golden. Remove with a slotted spoon and drain on paper towels. Sprinkle with salt.

To serve: Arrange on individual plates as illustrated, or place separately on a serving platter.

BACON, ONION AND JARLSBERG QUICHE

– 4 - 6 SERVINGS –

1 deep-dish frozen pie shell

FILLING:
150 g (5 oz) slab or 6 strips bacon
1 onion
1 tablespoon butter
100g (4 oz) mature Jarlsberg cheese (about 1 cup, grated)
2 tablespoons chopped parsley
2 dl (1 cup) whipping cream
2 dl (3/4 cup) milk
2 eggs
salt and pepper

Preheat the oven to 180C (350F). Defrost the pie shell. Line with baking parchment, fill with dried peas or rice (to hold the crust down) and bake 10-15 minutes. Remove the peas (can be reused) and bake 5 minutes more, until golden. Lower the heat to 170C (325F).

FILLING: Cut the bacon into cubes and blanch in boiling water. Drain. Peel and thinly slice the onion. Sauté in butter until transparent. Combine bacon and onion and sprinkle over the bottom of the pre-baked pie shell. Grate the Jarlsberg cheese on the fine side of the grater and arrange over the bacon. Sprinkle with parsley. Whisk cream, milk and eggs. Season with salt and pepper. Pour over the cheese.

Bake until set, 15-20 minutes. Serve lukewarm with a green salad.

Cold Rhubarb-Strawberry Soup

- 4 SERVINGS -

200 g (8 oz, 2-3 medium stalks) rhubarb
2 dl (1 cup) water
1 dl (1/2 cup) sugar
1/2 vanilla bean, split lengthwise
1 small cinnamon stick
200 g (8 oz, about 1 1/2 cups) strawberries
1 tablespoon chopped fresh lemon thyme

Clean the rhubarb and slice on the diagonal into 1 cm (1/2 in) pieces.
Bring water, sugar, vanilla and cinnamon to a boil. Lower heat and simmer 10 minutes. Add the rhubarb. As soon as it begins to bubble, remove from the heat. Cool overnight, without stirring.

Clean and quarter the strawberries. Add to the soup. Sprinkle with lemon thyme.

TO SERVE: Divide soup among four deep bowls. Top with vanilla ice cream or whipped cream and flaked hazelnuts.

SØRLANDET
summer in the south, seafood and shellfish

The southern coast is Norway's Riviera. Most of us associate this part of Norway with vacations, leisure time, boats and bathing. The sea provides a rich selection of its bounty, and good meals are usually synonymous with seafood – often served in the idyllic archipelago with fresh sea breezes, salty air and lush green foliage. Sørlandet has long seafaring traditions. Because of this, coastal towns and settlements were influenced from outside, and they got their continental atmosphere early. At any rate, compared with the rest of Norway.

LIVELY YET IDYLLIC
Today, towns along the coast of southern Norway dot the sea like pearls on a string. Well-maintained clapboard houses, blooming rose gardens behind white picket fences, lively small boat harbors, idyllic outdoor cafes and most of all, beaches for swimming and sunbathing. That's how we think of the southern part of Norway. The Norwegian coastal landscape is full of "light moments." Beautifully maintained places, developed by nature and by the people who have cared for these resources for centuries.

But this part of the country also has inland regions with towns, lakes and game. Beaver and moose were and are part of the diet here. And the people in these districts were without the coastal population's contact with the outside world. The food and the lifestyle were more local. Dishes were composed of ingredients near at hand. There's a lot of moose, together with a certain amount of freshwater fish and some beaver, as well as beef and veal from the farms.

Dishes with names like "bits and pieces" show that most was made according to the principle "use what you have."

Food eaten with a spoon was an important part of the Norwegian diet. And it doesn't take much imagination to understand the pleasure invoked by the aroma coming from a steaming pot filled with gifts from the sea or a game stew in the cottages of old. Traditional fish soups with something on the side are still favorites in the southern part of Norway.

MACKEREL AND MOOSE
Mackerel spawn along the Norwegian coast in April and May.

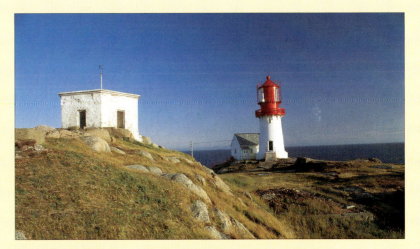

Afterwards, the large schools divide into smaller groups. They spend the summer dining on herring and become lovely fat fall mackerel before they swim off in September. Mackerel will always have a special place in the hearts of Norwegians (at least in those Norwegians from the southern part of the country). We go around waiting for it to come in the spring. They we set the table for a festive meal of fried mackerel and rhubarb soup. During the summer, we eat it cold and pickled, while in the fall, we often eat it poached, in stews and soups. Mackerel in Norway is sold fresh, frozen, salted, smoked and canned.

A moose carcass weighing more than 200 kilos (440 pounds) is a lot of food. That's why the moose always has been attractive game, and that goes for the moose in Sørlandet, too. Today, the moose population is large, and that means meat for the stewpot. Hunting is important for many, but the experience is just as important as the food nowadays. Using nature's surplus of game in a sensible way is part of Norwegian tradition. In addition, moose sauerbraten and moose stew with mushrooms are delicious.

Name:
Trond Moi
DOB:
December 28, 1969
Present Position:
Chef de Cuisine and restaurateur, "Bølgen & Moi," Oslo.
Previous Positions:
Stagier at Michel Guerard, France; cook at Holbergs Årstidene, Oslo; chef, The Norwegian Culinary Institute, Stavanger.
Awards:
In addition to the many gold and silver medals with the Norwegian Culinary Team: Gold - Norwegian Championships for chefs 1995; Fish chef of the year 1995; Gold - Nordic team championships 1995.

TROND MOI
– food, culture and art

The world-renowned Henie-Onstad Art Center at Høvik, right on the Oslo fjord, is about 20 minutes by car from Oslo. During the short time it's been there, the restaurant "Bølgen & Moi" has made quite a name for itself. And word is spreading about Trond Moi's food, especially the kind he serves in connection with new exhibitions.

What are your thoughts about food?

My goal is to combine food with culture, especially with regard to art. Food is art. Flavor, appearance and new, exciting combinations are important. I also am concerned about preserving our own traditions, renewing then and using them in modern food preparation.

What about Norwegian products?

Foods which grow naturally in Norway are among the best in the world. I am thinking about fish and vegetables here. Norwegian lamb is also some of the best meat we have. Norwegian butter too is of high quality. The culinary team take it with them on all their trips abroad. It has happened that master chefs from other countries ask to "borrow" a bit of our butter during competitions. Norwegian butter has export potential - for quality's sake.

What are your favorite dishes?

I like simply prepared, but spicy food, preferably with an Asian touch. And I love wonderful desserts.

Do you have your own style of cooking?

Yes, I really do. I like to make informal, modern food with a touch of "new world cuisine." I like to combine flavors and techniques from different cultures.

Why did you become a chef?

Because I wanted a job where I could develop creatively and learn all the time. Now I know that I have chosen a kind of lifestyle! In the beginning, it was the generous servings of hearty, flavorful rustic food, as well as the effective methods of preservation and traditions of the Norwegian kitchen which attracted me.

Do you have time for any other interests?

As I said earlier, being a chef is a lifestyle choice, at any rate for someone as interested and curious as I am. It's just food and more food - every day, when I'm traveling and when I'm studying - often combined with art!

What is the most important thing to you?

Enjoying what I do, to be happy while working and developing. But the most important thing to me? That's Line! (Trond Moi just got married.)

Do you cook at home?

Yes, I love to make food at home. What I make depends on the mood and the occasion, but I think it's both relaxing and fun.

How do you view the future?

I want to continue working to elevate the prestige and recognition of food as culture. I look forward to the time when most Norwegians feel that good food is an important part of life.

PICKLED MACKEREL WITH SUMMER VEGETABLES
– 4 SERVINGS –

2 dl (3/4 cup) water
2 dl (3/4 cup) white wine vinegar
2 dl (3/4 cup) sugar
3 bay leaves
1 teaspoon coriander seeds
1 teaspoon mustard seeds
1 teaspoon black peppercorns
1 teaspoon cloves
500 g (1 1/4 lbs) boneless but not skinless mackerel fillets

VEGETABLES:
2 scallions
2 carrots
4 asparagus stalks
16 snow peas
4 shallots
1 head oak leaf lettuce
1 tablespoon chopped chives
1 tablespoon chopped parsley

VINAIGRETTE:
1 dl (scant 1/2 cup) olive oil
1 teaspoon Dijon mustard
1/2 dl (3 tablespoons) wine vinegar
salt and pepper

HERB DRESSING:
1 1/2 dl (2/3 cup) dairy sour cream
juice of 1 lemon
2 tablespoons sugar
2 tablespoons minced parsley
2 tablespoons chopped chives
1 tablespoon chopped fresh basil
salt and pepper

Bring water, vinegar, sugar, bay leaves, coriander, mustard seed, peppercorns and cloves to a boil. Simmer over low heat about 5 minutes. Cut the fish into 3 cm (1 1/4 in) slices and place in the warm brine. Remove from the heat and cool completely.

VEGETABLES: Clean, peel and cut the vegetables into small even slices or pieces. Keep the asparagus whole. Parboil all vegetables in lightly salted water about 2 minutes. Plunge immediately into ice water. Drain. Wash the lettuce and tear into pieces.

VINAIGRETTE: Whisk all ingredients together and season with salt and pepper.

HERB DRESSING: Combine all ingredients well. Season with salt and pepper.

TO SERVE: Remove fish from the brine and drain. Arrange on four dinner plates. Arrange lettuce and vegetables over the fish. Sprinkle with chives and parsley. Drizzle vinaigrette over the vegetables. Spoon the herb dressing around the fish. Garnish with fresh herbs.

MACKEREL BURGERS WITH COLD RHUBARB SOUP
- 4 SERVINGS -

RHUBARB SOUP:
3 rhubarb stalks
5 dl (2 cups) water
170 g (scant 1 cup) sugar
1/2 vanilla bean
juice of 1 lemon
2 tablespoons chopped fresh mint

BURGERS:
2 large mackerel
1 1/2 dl (scant 2/3 cup) dairy sour cream
1 dl (scant 1/2 cup) chopped chives
1 tablespoon flour
3 rusks, crushed (or 1/2 cup dry bread crumbs)
1/4 teaspoon grated nutmeg
1 tablespoon butter

SAUCE:
150 g (5 oz, 5/8 cup) unsalted butter
1 dl (scant 1/2 cup) dairy sour cream (do not use low fat)
juice of 1 lemon
1 tablespoon chopped fresh chervil
1 tablespoon chopped chives
1 tablespoon chopped parsley

VEGETABLES:
3 carrots
1 leek
2 tablespoons butter

SOUP: Peel the rhubarb and cut into thin slices. Place the rhubarb peelings in a saucepan with the water, sugar, vanilla bean and lemon juice. Let steep about 10 minutes. Strain and add mint and rhubarb pieces. Bring to a boil, remove from the heat and cool completely.

BURGERS: Fillet the fish, removing all skin and bones. Rinse under running cold water and dry well with paper towels. Cut the fish into chunks, place in a food processor and pulse several times to make a coarse farce. Add sour cream, chives, flour and rusks. Season with salt, pepper and nutmeg. Form into burgers and fry in butter until golden and cooked through.

SAUCE: Brown the butter in the same pan. Add sour cream and lemon juice. Stir in the fresh herbs.

VEGETABLES: Wash and peel the carrots and clean the leek. Shred. Blanch in lightly salted water about 1 minute. Drain, then add butter, stirring so it melts. Season with salt and pepper.

TO SERVE: Arrange mackerel burgers on four heated dinner plates with vegetables and sauce. Serve with boiled potatoes. Serve soup ice cold alongside.

BAKED HALIBUT
WITH LEMON THYME SAUCE
– 4 SERVINGS –

800 g (1 3/4 lbs) boneless and skinless halibut
salt and pepper
1 teaspoon chopped basil
1 teaspoon chopped chives
1 teaspoon minced parsley

2 red bell peppers
100 g (4 oz) snow peas
1-2 tablespoons butter

100 g (4 oz, about 2/3 cup) pitted black olives
1/2 dl (3 tablespoons) olive oil

SAUCE:
1 shallot
1 tablespoon butter
1 dl (scant 1/2 cup) white wine
2 dl (3/4 cup) fish stock
2 dl (3/4 cup) whipping cream
salt and pepper
2 tablespoons chopped fresh lemon thyme

Preheat the oven to 170C (350F). Divide the fish into 4 pieces of equal size and arrange in a greased baking dish. Sprinkle with salt, pepper and chopped herbs. Bake 10-15 minutes.

Clean the peppers and snow peas. Cut into strips. Sauté in butter about 1 minute.

Puree olives and oil in a food processor until smooth. Season with salt and pepper

SAUCE: Chop the shallot and sauté in butter. Add wine and reduce until syrupy. Add stock (from cooking the fish plus more, as necessary) and cream and cook until somewhat thickened. Season with salt, pepper and lemon thyme.

TO SERVE: Place the fish on four dinner plates with the vegetables all around. Spoon sauce and olive puree around the fish. Serve with boiled potatoes.

Salad with Smoked Jarlsberg Cheese and Marinated Eggplant
- 4 servings -

Marinated eggplant:
1 eggplant
1 dl (1/3 cup) olive oil
1 small onion
1 garlic clove
1 dl (scant 1/2 cup) chopped canned tomatoes
1 tablespoon tomato paste

4 asparagus
2 tomatoes
1 head oak leaf lettuce
1 snake cucumber
2 ripe avocados
2 scallions
1 red bell pepper
2 tablespoons chopped chives
2 tablespoons chopped basil
salt and pepper
400 g (14 oz) smoked Jarlsberg

Basil dressing:
1 dl (1/3 cup) water
1 dl (1/3 cup) olive oil
1/2 large bunch basil
salt and pepper

Sour cream dressing:
1 1/2 dl (2/3 cup) light sour cream
1/2 dl (3 tablespoons) milk
1 tablespoon chopped chives
1 tablespoon minced parsley
1 tablespoon lemon juice
1 teaspoon sugar
salt and pepper

Marinated eggplant: Wash and dry the eggplant and cut into 1/2 cm (1/4 in) slices. Fry in olive oil or brush with oil and grill until cooked through. Transfer to a bowl. Peel and chop the onion and garlic. Stir in the chopped tomatoes, tomato paste, salt and pepper to taste. Pour over the eggplant slices and mix well.

Peel the asparagus and blanch 1 minute. Cut an "x" at the stem end of each tomato. Dip in boiling water about 30 seconds. Transfer immediately with a slotted spoon to ice water. Peel and slice. Wash the lettuce and tear it into small pieces. Wash/trim/peel the cucumber, avocado, scallions and bell pepper and cut into 1 cm (1/2 in) cubes or pieces. Combine vegetables, chives and basil. Season with salt and pepper.

Basil sauce: Puree water, olive oil and basil in a food processor or blender until smooth. Season with salt and pepper.

Sour cream sauce: Combine all ingredients and season with salt and pepper to taste.

Cut the cheese into 2 mm slices.

To serve: Arrange in layers on four dinner plates, in the following order: Cheese, marinated eggplant slices, lettuce, mixed vegetables and herbs. Lean the asparagus against the salad. Garnish with herbs. Spoon the two sauces around the layered salad. Serve with crusty bread.

Filet of Veal with Rosemary and Jarlsberg Scalloped Potatoes

- 4 servings -

800 g (1 3/4 lbs) veal tenderloin
salt and pepper
3 tablespoons chopped rosemary
2 tablespoons olive oil

16 tiny carrots
4 scallions
1 small head new cabbage
2 tablespoons butter
2 tablespoons minced parsley

Tarragon jus:
2 shallots
2 tablespoons butter
5 dl (2 cups) heavily reduced veal stock
3 tablespoons butter
salt and pepper
4 tablespoons (1/4 cup) chopped fresh tarragon

Jarlsberg scalloped potatoes:
about 500 g (1 1/4 lbs) almond (or other waxy) potatoes
1 garlic clove
1 dl (1/2 cup) milk
2 dl (3/4 cup) whipping cream
salt and pepper
200 g (1 3/4 cups) grated Jarlsberg cheese

Tarragon jus: Peel and chop shallots and sauté in butter. Add stock and bring to a boil. Season with salt and pepper. Just before serving, stir in tarragon.

Jarlsberg scalloped potatoes: Peel and slice potatoes and mince the garlic. Place in the saucepan with the milk and cream. Bring to a boil, stirring carefully. Simmer until potatoes are soft. Preheat the oven to 220C (425F). Season with salt and pepper. Transfer to an oven proof dish. Sprinkle with cheese. Bake until the cheese is melted and golden brown, 5-8 minutes.

To serve: Cut the meat into even slices and divide among four dinner plates. Arrange vegetables around meat. Spoon on the tarragon-flavored juices. Serve the potatoes directly from the casserole.

Preheat the oven to 180C (350F). Trim all fat and membrane from meat. Season with salt, pepper and rosemary. Brown on all sides in oil. Transfer to a baking tray and roast 15 minutes. Let the meat rest at least 10 minutes before slicing.

Wash carrots, slice scallions into 3. The new cabbage in cloves. Cook the cabbage in salted water for 3 minutes, carrots and scallions for 1 minute. Before serving, put on the butter and minced parsley.

— 105 —

HADDOCK QUENELLES WITH CURRIED JARLSBERG SAUCE
- 4 servings -

400 g (14 oz) boneless and skinless haddock fillet
1 teaspoon salt
2 tablespoons butter
1 egg
3 dl (1 1/4 cups) creme fraiche or dairy sour cream (do not use low-fat)
salt and pepper

2 zucchini
2 carrots
1 tablespoon olive oil

CURRIED JARLSBERG SAUCE:
2 shallots
3 tablespoons butter
1/2 teaspoon curry powder
2 tablespoons flour
2 dl (3/4 cup) milk (do not use low-fat)
3 dl (1 1/4 cups) fish stock
150 g (5 oz) Jarlsberg cheese

Cut the fish into chunks and place in a food processor with the salt. Puree until smooth. Add egg, mixing well. With the motor running, add creme fraiche. Season with salt and pepper. Form into ovals. Bring lightly salted water to a boil. Place the balls in the water with a spoon. Poach about 5 minutes. Drain.

Wash, trim and slice the zucchini. Sauté lightly in olive oil. Peel the carrots, cut into batons and cook in lightly salted water until crisp tender. Drain, then coat with butter.

SAUCE: Mince the shallot and sauté in butter with the curry powder. Add the flour, stirring well. Whisk in milk and stock. Simmer 5-10 minutes. Cut the cheese into small cubes. Just before serving, add the cubes to the sauce, stirring until melted. Season with salt and pepper.

TO SERVE: Divide the quenelles among four dinner plates. Arrange the vegetables on top. Spoon sauce all around. Serve with potatoes.

— 107 —

Veiled Southern Girls (Apple Compote with Chocolate and Spiced Plums)
- 4 servings -

4 apples
2 tablespoons butter
3 tablespoons sugar
1/4 teaspoon ground cinnamon

HAZELNUT PRALINE:
50 g (1/4 cup) sugar
100 g (4 oz, 1 cup) hazelnuts
1/4 teaspoon ground cinnamon

SPICED PLUMS:
4 plums
3 dl (1 1/4 cups) water
3 dl (1 1/4 cups) sugar
1/2 vanilla bean
1 cinnamon stick

2 dl (3/4 cup) whipping cream
1 teaspoon confectioner's sugar

100 g (4 oz) semi-sweet chocolate

Peel and core the apple. Cut into even wedges. Melt the butter and stir in sugar and cinnamon. Add apples and cook until caramelized. Cool to room temperature.

HAZELNUT PRALINE: Melt the sugar and cook until caramelized. Do not burn. Mix in nuts and cinnamon. Cool, then crush into crumbs.

SPICED PLUMS: Combine all ingredients in a saucepan. Bring to a boil, lower heat and simmer until plums are tender. Cool.

Whip the cream with the confectioner's sugar.

Melt the chocolate in a double boiler or microwave oven.

TO SERVE: Brush the entire surface of deep dishes with melted chocolate. Drip over stripes of chocolate as illustrated. Layer cream, apples and praline in 4 glasses or bowls. Place these on dishes. Arrange plums on top. Garnish with melted chocolate and serve with raspberry sauce.

17TH OF MAY
- theres rejoicing everywhere

Many countries celebrate their national days with great military parades. In Norway, Constitution Day, May 17, is first and foremost a day of joy, especially for children! And for nature. At this time of year, the birch trees are in bloom and fields and woods are turning green. It is said that not even the American or the French independence days are infused with such enthusiasm as Norway's own yearly celebration. It was on this day in 1814 that our forefathers signed our nation's Constitution at Eidsvoll. After World War II, the word "freedom" and our celebration of it became extra meaningful.

CHILDREN'S PARADES AND TRUMPET MUSIC

In the capital of Oslo, there's a giant children's parade up Karl Johans gate, the main street. The goal is to wave to Norway's King Harald and Queen Sonja and their family on the balcony of the royal palace. People march in parades throughout the country, swinging Norwegian flags and shouting "hurrah." Everyone who owns one puts on a "bunad," (traditional regional costume) or other fancy dress. May 17 is the day for children's parades, regional dress, nationwide speeches and a big party for everyone! A special feature is the many marching bands. Boys and girls play Norwegian songs and marches as they parade in their colorful uniforms. Both the children and the music make the celebration extra festive.

Between the events on this long, rather tiring day, children fill up on hot dogs, ice cream, candy and soda. For grown-ups, May 17th is a day for "eggedosis" (a kind of thick eggnog made without liquid), a fine dinner, wonderful desserts and Norwegian cream cakes.

FESTIVE NORWEGIAN FOOD

Cake and coffee have strong traditions in Norwegian food culture. Many good cakes are baked in home kitchens all over Norway. Especially before festive occasions and holidays. And there's no skimping on the ingredients. Eggs, butter, cream and good Norwegian berries and fruit are and always will be the main ingredients. And all Norwegian homes have their own specialty cakes. There are, by the way, great variations from district to district and from family to family.

In Norway, it has always been the tradition that important holidays and special family occasions are celebrated with a festive meal. That's part of a good social life, as on May 17th, and when we grill in the garden or present a dinner with many courses (often with new spring vegetables, salmon and strawberries) or make a traditional Norwegian buffet.

CURED MEAT, BEER AND AQUAVIT

Cured meats have always been festive food in Norway. On a May 17th table, you often can find cured ham and dried leg of mutton, a variety of sausages and flatbreads, both crisp and soft. Side dishes include scrambled eggs with chives, sour cream, creamed potatoes or potato salad. Beer and aquavit accompany this kind of festive food.

For dessert, gelatin and Bavarian creams appear on most tables, along with compotes, ice cream and puddings, of which caramel, chocolate and Madeira are good examples. In addition, Norway is richly endowed with delicious berries from both field and forest.

Name:
   NINA SJØEN
DOB:
   August 9, 1961
Present Position:
   Pastry Chef, Tante Sofies Hus, Oslo (from October, 1996).
Previous Positions:
   Cook, Restaurant Blom, Oslo 1985-86; cook/dessert chef, Spisestedet Feinschmecker, Oslo 1986-90. Dessert chef Restaurant Bagatelle, Oslo 1990-95.
   Practice from Le Gavroche, London and Westin Stanford, Singapore; also worked in Malaysia and New Zealand.
Awards:
   A number of medals with the Norwegian Culinary Team.

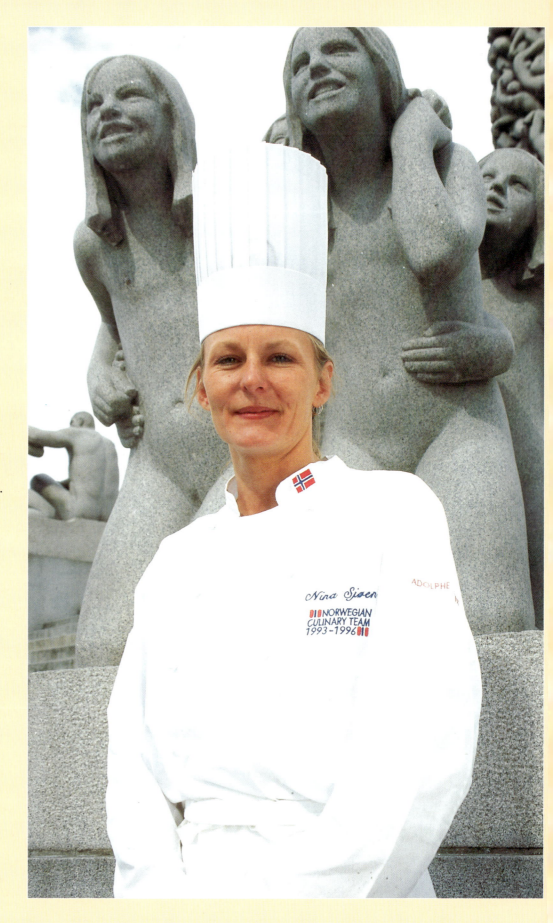

NINA SJØEN
- the only chicken in the culinary team basket

When we read newspaper headlines about medals and honors won by the Norwegian Culinary Team, there is a woman making the most fantastic desserts together with Lars Lian. But she has also run the dessert kitchen with a firm hand at the prestigious Restaurant Bagatelle in Oslo, among other things...

A little about your food philosophy.

There's no doubt. I like making desserts best. Colors, decoration, flavor and harmony. I like detail work, you have to realize, and I have a lot of patience. I want a superb dessert to be at least as important as the other courses in a meal. It is a pleasure to work with top quality, pure raw materials.

What about Norwegian ingredients?

We have to learn to appreciate our good products, store and age them correctly. In addition, in our modern world with short distances to anywhere and everywhere, we should import what we don't have, or if what we do have isn't good enough. The combination of Norwegian and foreign in exciting and harmonious ways is the goal. Other countries also should have access to our "treasures." Strawberries and cherries are some. Norwegian cream and sour cream are wonderful texture and flavor enhancers in Norwegian cooking and baking.

What do you enjoy eating?

Grilled prawns with garlic butter as served at the "Sardine Factory" in California are a favorite. Otherwise, I like hearty Norwegian home cooked food, and I am just as big a fan of oriental dishes. Maybe because both are so remote from my daily dessert acrobatics.

Do you have your own style?

It must be to create modern desserts and baked goods with Norwegian ingredients, and bring in the foreign when necessary or best. I am well anchored in the French and central European style and tradition, but in my own way...

Why did you choose this kind of a career?

I couldn't sit still! After business school, I ended up behind a desk solving math problems. I felt the need for other kinds of challenges, and I wanted to move around more. I have always been interested in food, and I enjoy preparing it. So food became my profession.

Do you have time for any other interests?

Most of my time involves food. Much of my "leisure time" is used training and perfecting with the culinary team. But I like to travel. My profession has taken me to many countries in different parts of the world - France, USA, New Zealand, Thailand. And I worked in Singapore for a month.

What is the most important thing for you?

It is important to be constantly developing, creating new things and combinations - all for the pleasure of the guests.

What about your home kitchen?

There's less time for cooking at home than I'd really like. Sometimes I even eat Christmas pork during the summer. Then I know I have time for it.

17th of May Cake

Grand Marnier sponge base:
6 eggs
190 g (2 1/4 dl, scant 1 cup) sugar
175 g (3 dl, 1 1/4 cup) flour
1 tablespoon potato starch (or cornstarch)
1 teaspoon baking powder
2 tablespoons Grand Marnier (or other orange-flavored) liqueur

Banana-lime cream:
2 vanilla beans
4 dl (1 2/3 cups) milk
(do not use low-fat)
150 g (1 3/4 dl, 3/4 cup) sugar
5 egg yolks
40 g (3/4 dl, 1/3 cup) cornstarch
2 bananas
juice of 2 limes
1 dl (1/2 cup) wipping cream

1 liter (quart) whipping cream
1 - 1 1/2 dl (1/2 - 2/3 cup)
creme fraiche or dairy sour cream
(do not use low-fat)
1/2 kg (1 lb, about 3 cups) strawberries, rinsed, topped and sliced
milk

Banana-lime cream: Split the vanilla beans lengthwise and scrape out the seeds. Place beans and seeds with milk and sugar in a saucepan. Bring to a boil. Whisk egg yolks with cornstarch in a bowl. Whisk in the warm milk, then pour back into the saucepan. Heat to boiling. Remove vanilla beans. Pour into a food processor. Peel and slice bananas and add with lime juice. Puree until smooth. Refrigerate until cold. Fold in wipped cream.

Whip the cream until it clots. Whip the cream fraiche (it thins out first, then peaks). Fold the two creams lightly together. Divide the sponge horizontally into 3 layers. Sprinkle with milk. Layer with banana-lime cream, strawberries and whipped cream/creme fraiche. Spoon remaining cream into a pastry tube and decorate the cake as desired. Garnish with strawberries.

Preheat the oven to 180C (350F). Grease and flour a 24 cm (9 in) springform pan. Beat eggs and sugar until thick and lemon-colored. Combine dry ingredients and sift over egg mixture. Fold lightly but thoroughly. Stir in the liqueur. Pour into the prepared pan. Bake until the cake pulls away from the sides of the pan, about 40 minutes.

Passion Fruit Cheesecake

Nut sponge base:
4 egg whites
200 g (2 1/2 dl, 1 cup) sugar
260 g (6 dl, 2 1/2 cups) finely ground almonds

Passion fruit cream:
500 g (18 oz) natural cream cheese
325 g (3 3/4 dl, 1 2/3 cups) sugar
5 sheets (teaspoons) unflavored gelatin
juice of 2 limes
1 1/2 - 2 dl (2/3-3/4 cup) passion fruit concentrate (or orange juice concentrate)
6 1/2 dl (2 2/3 cups) whipping cream

Gelatin topping:
150 g (5 oz, about 1 1/4 dl, 1/2 cup) passion fruit concentrate (or orange juice concentrate)
75 g (3/4 dl, 1/3 cup) sugar
1 1/2 dl (2/3 cup) water
30 g (1 oz, about 1 1/2 tablespoons) glucose
4 1/2 sheets (2 teaspoons) unflavored gelatin
1 teaspoon cornstarch

Nut sponge base: Preheat the oven to 200C (400F). Beat egg whites with sugar until stiff and glossy. Fold in the nuts lightly but thoroughly. Pour into a 25 cm (10 in) springform pan. Bake about 15 minutes.

Passion fruit cream: Beat cream cheese and sugar in a food processor until smooth. Soak gelatin sheets in cold water (Sprinkle powdered gelatin over lime juice) to soften, about 10 minutes. Squeeze excess water from gelatin sheets (disregard for powdered gelatin). Melt in the lime juice. Stir in passion fruit concentrate, stirring well. Add to the cheese mixture. Whip the cream and fold into the cheese mixture. Pour over the nut sponge. Freeze.

Gelatin topping: Bring passion fruit concentrate, sugar, water and glucose to a boil. Skim well. Soak gelatin sheets in cold water (Sprinkle powdered gelatin over 2 tablespoons cold water) to soften. Stir cornstarch into 1 teaspoon water. Stir into fruit mixture and simmer 2-3 minutes. Squeeze excess water from gelatin sheets (disregard for powdered gelatin). Melt gelatin in fruit mixture. Refrigerate until it begins to set. Spread over cake in a thin layer. Refrigerate.

To serve: Decorate as illustrated.

Crispy Almond Cookies

260 g (4 dl, 1 2/3 cups) blanched almonds
120 g (1 1/2 dl, 2/3 cup) sugar
2 eggs
20 g (3 tablespoons) cornstarch
about 1 dl (scant 1/2 cup) milk

Preheat the oven to 190C (375F). Finely grind the nuts in a food processor. Add sugar, eggs, cornstarch and milk. Brush the mixture over a parchment-lined baking sheet into thin 3x10 cm (1 1/4x4 in) lengths (use a template). Bake until golden, about 4 minutes.

ANISE PARFAIT
- 8 SERVINGS -

ALMOND MACAROONS:
2 dl (7/8 cup) egg whites
25 g (2 tablespoons) sugar
100 g (2 dl, 7/8 cup) confectioner's sugar
50 g (1 1/4 dl, 1/2 cup) finely ground almonds

ANISE PARFAIT:
20 g (3/4 oz, 3/4 dl, 1/3 cup) whole star anise
100 g (1 1/4 dl, 1/2 cup) sugar
1 dl (scant 1/2 cup) water
6 egg yolks
1/2 dl (3 tablespoons) Pernod
3 1/2 dl (1 1/2 cups) whipping cream

CHOCOLATE KISSES:
5 egg whites
a few drops lemon juice
125 g (1 1/2 dl, 2/3 cup) sugar
125 g (2 dl, 7/8 cup) confectioner's sugar
2 1/2 tablespoons cocoa

STRAWBERRY SAUCE:
150 g (1 3/4 dl, 3/4 cup) sugar
juice of 1 lemon
juice of 1 orange
500 g (1 1/4 lb, about 3 cups cleaned) fresh strawberries

ALMOND MACAROONS: Preheat the oven to 175C (350F). Beat egg whites with sugar until stiff and glossy. Combine confectioner's sugar and nuts. Fold into the egg white mixture lightly but thoroughly. Spoon into a pastry bag. Pipe macaroons onto a parchment covered baking sheet. Bake 15 minutes. Remove from the baking sheet and place in individual molds.

ANISE PARFAIT: Simmer star anise, sugar and water 5 minutes. Strain to remove anise. Bring to a boil and cook until thicker (121C, 250F) on a candy thermometer. Beat egg yolks in a food processor until light. Add the hot sugar syrup all at once. Beat until cool. Add Pernod. Whip the cream and fold in carefully. Pour over the macaroons in their molds. Freeze.

CHOCOLATE KISSES:
Preheat the oven to 100C (210F). Beat egg whites until stiff. Gradually add lemon juice and sugar and beat until stiff and glossy. Combine confectioner's sugar and cocoa. Fold into the egg white mixture lightly but thoroughly, until shiny again. Spoon into a pastry bag. Pipe kisses onto a parchment covered baking sheet. Bake about 45 minutes.

STRAWBERRY SAUCE:
Bring sugar, lemon and orange juices to a boil. Simmer 2 minutes to make a sugar syrup. Wash and clean strawberries. Place in a food processor. Add syrup and puree. Strain.

TO SERVE: Unmold parfaits and place on flat dishes. Garnish as illustrated.

BAKED APPLES IN FILO
– (4 SERVINGS) –

4 apples
1 tablespoon brown sugar
2 tablespoons sugar
2 tablespoons raisins
30 g (1 oz, 3/4 dl, 1/3 cup) chopped nuts
1/2 teaspoon ground cinnamon
2 tablespoons toasted crumbs (cookies or white toast)
filo pastry
clarified unsalted butter

CARAMEL-WHISKY SAUCE:
200 g (7 oz) sugar lumps
1 dl (scant 1/2 cup) whipping cream
3 1/2 dl (1 1/2 cups) milk
6 egg yolks
2-3 tablespoons Scotch whisky

GINGER CREAM:
3 dl (1 1/4 cups) creme fraiche or dairy sour cream
1 1/2 teaspoons grated fresh ginger
30 g (2 1/2 tablespoons) sugar

Preheat the oven to 200C (400F). Clean, peel, core and cube apples. Combine with both sugars, raisins, nuts, cinnamon and crumbs. Wrap 1/4 of the apple mixture in 2 sheets filo pastry. Repeat 3 more times. Brush with clarified butter and place on a parchment covered baking sheet. Bake 15-20 minutes until golden.

SAUCE: Add the sugar lumps to a hot pan. Caramelize until they fizz. Add cream and milk and bring to a boil. Beat egg yolks in a bowl. Pour over cream mixture in a thin stream, stirring constantly. Heat carefully, stirring constantly, until thickened. Strain, then stir in the whisky. Cool quickly by placing the pan in ice water.

GINGER CREAM: Combine all ingredients in a saucepan and bring to a boil. Cool. Press through a sieve. Whip (as with cream).

TO SERVE: Serve the apple packets warm. Top with scoops of ginger cream and a sprinkle of cinnamon. Serve the sauce alongside.

WARM CHOCOLATE TART WITH COCONUT SAUCE

- (3 tarts) -

BASE:
125 g (4 1/2 oz, 1/2 cup + 1 tablespoon) unsalted butter, softened
235 g (3 3/4 dl, 1 2/3 cups) flour
100 g (2 dl, 7/8 cup) confectioner's sugar
40 g (1 dl, scant 1/2 cup) finely ground almonds

CHOCOLATE SOUFFLÉ:
100 g (3 1/2 oz, 1/2 cup - 1 tablespoon)
150 g (5 1/2 oz) semi-sweet chocolate
2 eggs
2 egg yolks
30 g (2 1/2 tablespoons) sugar

COCONUT SAUCE:
2 sheets (1 teaspoon) unflavored gelatin
4 dl (1 2/3 cups) cream of coconut
1 tablespoon sugar
1 dl (scant 1/2 cup) whipping cream

BASE: Preheat the oven to 180C (350F). Combine butter and flour in a food processor. Add flour and nuts and pulse quickly until the dough just holds together. Wrap in plastic and refrigerate 1 hour. Divide into thirds and roll out each to fit a 16 cm (6 in) springform pan. Place in the freezer about 15 minutes before baking. Bake until golden, about 8 minutes.

SOUFFLÉ: Preheat the oven to 220F (425C). Melt butter and chocolate in a double boiler or in the microwave. Cool. Beat eggs, egg yolks and sugar until light and lemon-colored. Fold in the melted chocolate lightly but thoroughly. Divide the mixture among the 3 bases. Bake about 11 minutes.

SAUCE: Soak the gelatin sheets in cold water (sprinkle the powdered gelatin over 1 tablespoon of the cream of coconut) to soften, about 10 minutes. Squeeze excess water from the gelatin sheets (disregard for powdered gelatin). Melt in a small amount of the cream of coconut. Stir in the sugar and the remaining cream of coconut and heat well, stirring to distribute gelatin. Cool. Thin with cream.

TO SERVE: Cut the tarts into even pieces and place on flat dishes. Garnish as desired and serve the sauce alongside.

AUTUMN TART

To this delicious cake you use the same base as in the recipe; Chocolate tart

VANILLA CREAM:
1/2 l milk
2 vanilla beans
3 egg yolks
2 eggs
125 g sugar
50 g corn starch
125 g (unsalted) butter
1 cl Lakka (Cloudberries liqueur)

Garnish: Cloudberries

Bring milk, sugar and vanilla to a boil. Stir occasionally. Mix together the eggs and the corn starch. Add the hot milk, little by little. Stir. Have the mixture in the sauce pan and bring it to a boil. Cooking time, 2 minutes. Set aside to cool.

Wip the butter. Remove the vanilla beans from the mixture. Wip the vanilla cream. Fold the butter into the cream. Pour in the Lakka. Wip again.

Pour the cream into the cake base. Garnish it with cloudberries.

Norwegian cookies

Brown Cookies
Yield: about 40

125 g (4 oz, 1/2 cup) unsalted butter
125 g (1 1/2 dl, 2/3 cup) sugar
1 1/2 tablespoons syrup
1/2 teaspoon potash stirred into 1 teaspoon water
225 g (3 3/4 dl, 1 2/3 cups) flour
30 g (1 oz, 3/4 dl, 1/3 cup) finely ground blanched almonds
1/2 teaspoon ground cloves
1 1/2 teaspoon ground cinnamon
50 g (3/4 dl, 1/3 cup) chopped candied orange peel

Bring butter, sugar and syrup to the boiling point. Add potash-water mixture. Cool to lukewarm and add remaining ingredients. Combine to make a smooth dough. Form into rolls (3 1/2 cm, 1 1/2 in diameter). Wrap in plastic and refrigerate overnight. Preheat the oven to 175C (350F). Cut into 3 mm (1/8 in) thick slices with a sharp knife. Place on a parchment covered baking sheet. Bake 5-7 minutes. Cool. These cookies keep well in an airtight tin.

Berlin Wreaths
Yield: about 40 cookies

1 hard cooked egg yolk
1 raw egg yolk
60 g (3/4 dl, 1/3 cup) sugar
125 g (4 oz, 1/2 cup) unsalted butter, softened
250 g (9 oz, 4 1/4 dl, 1 3/4 cups) flour
1 egg white, lightly beaten
chopped almonds
pearl sugar (or crushed sugar cubes)

Mash the cooked yolk with the raw. Add sugar and beat until thick and lemon-colored. Alternately beat in butter and flour for a smooth dough. Wrap in plastic, then refrigerate 1 hour. Preheat the oven to 190C (375F). Roll the dough to finger-thick sausages. Cut into 10 cm (4 in) lengths. Form into wreaths with the ends crossing over one another. Brush with beaten egg white, then dip in chopped almonds and pearl sugar. Place on a parchment lined baking sheet and bake about 8 minutes. Cool. Store in an airtight tin.

Mor Monsen

250 g (9 oz, 1 cup) butter
250 g (3 dl, 1 1/4 cups) sugar
6 eggs
250 g (4 1/4 dl, 1 3/4 cups) flour
1 teaspoon baking powder
grated zest of 1 lemon
1 dl (1/2 cup) currants/raisins
1 dl (1/2 cup) chopped almonds
3 tablespoons pearl sugar (or crushed sugar cubes)

Preheat the oven to 180C (350F). Grease a 25x35 cm (10x15 in) pan. Beat butter and sugar until light and fluffy. Add eggs, one at a time, beating well after each, alternating with flour, baking powder and lemon zest. Pour into prepared pan. Sprinkle with currants/raisins, almonds and pearl sugar. Bake 30 minutes. Cool completely, then cut into neat squares. Store in an airtight tin or freeze.

Tuiles
Yield: about 50 cookies

100 g (3 1/2 oz, scant 1/2 cup) butter
150 g (3 dl, 1 1/4 cups) confectioner's sugar
4 egg whites
125 g (2 dl, 7/8 cup) flour
1 teaspoon vanilla sugar (1/2 teaspoon extract)
1 teaspoon cocoa

Preheat the oven to 200C (400F). Melt the butter, cool slightly. Stir in all remaining ingredients except cocoa. Remove 2 tablespoons batter and mix with cocoa. Spoon batter in thin 15 cm (6 in) circles on a greased baking sheet. Spoon the chocolate batter into a pastry tube and pipe a thin spiral on each cookie. Bake until golden, 5-6 minutes. Shape around a "krumkake" cone or cannoli tube as soon as they are removed from the oven. Cool. Store in an airtight tin.

Apricot Gems
Yield: about 40 cookies

Sweet pastry:
180 g (3 dl, 1 1/4 cups) flour
1 1/2 tablespoons sugar
125 g (4 oz, 1/2 cup) unsalted butter
1 egg yolk

Almond mixture:
200 g (4 3/4 dl, 2 cups) finely ground almonds
200 g (4 1/4 dl, 1 3/4 cups) confectioner's sugar
2 egg whites

200 g (7 oz, about 3/4 cup) very thick apricot preserves

Beat all ingredients together to make a smooth dough. Cover with plastic, then refrigerate at least 15 minutes. Preheat the oven to 185C (375F). Beat almonds, sugar and egg whites until thick. Remove the dough from the refrigerator and roll 3 mm (1/16 in) thick. Cut out round cookies with a cookie cutter or the top of a glass. Place on a greased baking sheet. Place the almond mixture in a pastry tube and pipe a ring around the edge of each cookie. Place 1 teaspoon apricot preserves in the center. Bake 10-15 minutes. Cool. Store in an airtight tin.

KRUMKAKES
YIELD: ABOUT 20

2 eggs
110 g (4 oz, 1/2 cup + 1 tablespoon) sugar
110 g (4 oz, 1/2 cup) unsalted butter
110 g (4 oz, scant 2 dl, 3/4 cup) flour
1/2 teaspoon cardamom

Beat eggs and sugar until light and lemon colored. Melt the butter and beat until cool (mayonnaise consistency). Add to egg mixture. Sift in flour and cardamom. Fold lightly together. Let rest 1 hour. Heat a "krumkake" iron (available at specialty shops - a pizzelle iron also can be used). Place 1 tablespoon batter on the iron. Bake until light golden. Form over cones or drape over cups to fill with berries. Store in an airtight tin. Handle carefully - they break easily.

COCONUT-GINGER MACAROONS
YIELD: 40 COOKIES

2 egg whites
125 g (1 1/2 dl, 2/3 cup) sugar
1/2 teaspoon baking powder
125 g (3 1/2 dl, 1 1/2 cups) flaked coconut
25 g (1 oz, 1/4 cup) chopped candied ginger

Preheat the oven to 175C (350F). Beat egg whites until stiff but not dry. Gradually add sugar. Stir in baking powder, coconut and ginger. Place spoonfuls of the mixture on a parchment lined baking sheet. Bake 10-12 minutes. Cool completely before removing from the parchment. Store in an airtight tin.

RØROS
- hunting, wilderness - and a gem of a town

We now are in central Norway. Femund lake territory, the Røros plateau, the mining town! In Norway, there are all kinds of adventures. "There's no place I'd rather freeze than here," is a familiar statement. Because in these parts, the thermometer easily drops to -30C (-22F). The record is -53C (-63F). But the light is a wonderful shade of pink, and it's like traveling into a Christmas card over the hard, frozen snow. Don't be surprised if you hear sleigh bells and have to pull aside to let a horse-drawn sleigh pass by...

People visit year-round to enjoy the great outdoors, hunting and fishing, and the mountain plateau and forests stretch as far as the eye can see, even further. Here you find competitive skiers in training, nature photographers, hunters, sports fishermen, dog team drivers, and hikers. If you're lucky, you can see musk oxen and wild or tame reindeer. There are many kinds of wilderness experiences - the swan songs of winter, the southern Sami with their flocks of reindeer, the lights and colors of autumn, sitting around the campfire by the water, sitting toasty warm under thick pelts on a sleigh ride over the snow, or a summer visit to the small farms high up on the plateau.

Here the traditional foods are taken seriously. Cured meats, sausages and dried fish, crispbread in great stacks. People are still carrying on these rich traditions from the Røros area. Good old-fashioned fare without additives are produced for sale. Here the natural ingredients are in focus, as they always have been. The settlements in the mountain have sustained themselves on game and fish from the open country, but also on milk and meat produced on their own farms.

THE MINING TOWN OF RØROS

is located on the mountain plateau, the town with the highest elevation in Norway. The search for metals and the establishment of the mine determined its location 650 meters (2535 feet) above sea level. There's been a settlement here since the middle of the 17th century, a combination of mining and farming town. People combined working at the mines with keeping stock. On the outskirts of town are grassy areas, small mountain dairy farms and outlying hayfields. The slag piles from copper mining are a characteristic feature of the town. All these are now protected areas. The three oldest buildings here date from the rebuilding after the fires of 1678-9. These give the town its distinct character.

And many houses are protected by law. In 1980, Røros was placed on UNESCO's list of historic monuments, and it has its own historian. The tall baroque church dominates the town. It seats 1500 and is a popular photo motif. Now in 1996, the mining town of Røros is celebrating its 350-year jubilee.

"To eat according to the size of the bowl" was both important and necessary here. Food had to be stretched to last through a long and cold winter. And that often meant "sul" or salted foods. It became

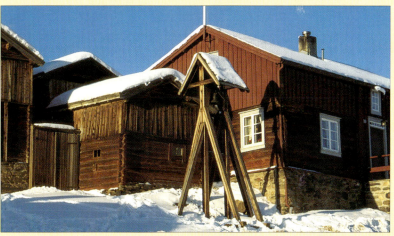

something of an art to find cheap available food to round out the menu. Flour and potatoes were a blessing in that way, because they could be used for many things. Frequently, porridge or gruel was served on its own. But now and then, there was a bit of bacon or a piece of dried meat for everyone, and the meal became a feast. Moderation was an absolute necessity here in the hills.

ITS OWN WINTER FESTIVAL

Røros market is a 139-year-old tradition. Every February, it draws thousands of visitors to the town. This is high season for cultural life. There's buying, singing and dancing for five days. Food is important, of course: there's grilling of goat and reindeer, exotic dishes from around the world, skilled local bakers giving out samples, sour sausages and sour cream porridge, all kinds of local breads. The region also has beaver, dried reindeer meat, smoked whitefish and cow udders on its list of specialties.

But today, the excellent products from Norway's richest hunting and fishing areas are used in modern ways. The world is always changing. But still, if you visit this gem of a town, you owe it to yourself to sample the coarsely ground sausage, rolled meat and salt pork, with mashed rutabagas and almond potatoes.

Name:
Jørn Lie
DOB:
May 27, 1969
Position:
Chef Cuisine at Spisestedet Feinschmecker in Oslo.
Previous Positions:
Apprentice, Grand Hotel, Oslo and later cook at the same hotel. 1988/90 cook at the Norwegian Pavillion, Epcot Center, Florida. Then Fossheim Turisthotel, Lom, cook under Arne Brimi. Pro 1991. Spisestedet Feinschmecker – starting as a cook, then assistant chef and from 1992 Chef Cuisine the same place.
Awards:
Some gold- and silvermedals with the Norwegian Culinary Team 1992/96, at Salon Culinare, Singapore and American Culinary Classic.

JØRN LIE
– a young and talented feinschmecker

You can find chef Jørn Lie at Spisestedet Feinschmecker
in Oslo, one of three Norwegian restaurants with Michelin stars!
And he doesn't work with just anyone, either; Lars Erik Underthun, one
of Norway's really high profile chefs, manages the restaurant.

Tell us a little about your food philosophy.

It is to make really good food from available raw materials. This is important – everything doesn't have to be expensive. Take, for example, good Norwegian root vegetables. By using different means of preparation, the different nuances in flavor are revealed.

What do you have to say about Norwegian products?

Some of our Norwegian ingredients are perhaps among the best in the world. But here – as in most countries – there are some things which aren't good enough. Here in Norway, for example, we don't have any proper classification system for meat for the consumer. That is unfortunate.

What do you like to eat?

I often feel that traditional dishes such as lamb and cabbage stew, Mom's meat cakes and fresh fish are the best. But truly, a good hot dog with mustard and fresh potato lumper (a tortilla-like soft flatbread made with potatoes and rye flour) hits the spot once in a while. And there are no better strawberries than our own!
For real enjoyment, there's nothing like ocean crayfish, asparagus or foie gras. But such things are rare.

Do you have your own style in the kitchen?

Yes, and I would like to call it "refined rustic food." The flavors are often hearty, preferably with a taste of Norway. I also try to find the best new and classic flavors from the international kitchen.

Why did you choose to become a chef?

I have always liked to use both my hands and my head doing something creative. By making food, you can "create" all the time, and you can see the results. There really are no limits – only those set by your imagination.

What are your interests?

Food – and reading cookbooks – are my main interest, often combined with listening to good music. I have a bit of "collectomania," especially when it comes to cookbooks and CD's.

Do you cook at home?

It's usually simpler things, like pasta dishes. When there's enough time, I like to cook good traditional food. If we have guests, I sometimes serve food similar to what I make at the restaurant, and sometimes I try out new ideas.

How do you view the future?

We have to preserve the traditions of the Norwegian kitchen, not try to make them something other than what they are. To preserve and maintain all that's clean and pure in nature is also important. Otherwise, we must maintain high standards of food preparation, to respect the craftsmanship behind it, and not let industry take over the profession. That's why we have to make flavorful food with the best products, in combination with the best sauces.

BARBECUE-SMOKED TROUT

– 4 SERVINGS –

800 g (1 3/4 lbs) boneless and skinless trout fillet

SMOKING:
*equal parts sugar and salt
aromatic wood chips*

MARINADE:
*2 tablespoons brown sugar
4 tablespoons (1/4 cup) tomato paste
2 tablespoons soy sauce
2 tablespoons tarragon vinegar
2 drops Louisiana hot pepper sauce
salt and freshly ground white pepper*

SAUCE:
*4 shallots
olive oil
5 dl (2 cups) dry white wine
200 g (7 oz, 7/8 cup) unsalted butter, softened
salt and freshly ground white pepper
1 bunch fresh cress, coarsely chopped*

VEGETABLES:
*1 small eggplant
5 dl (2 cups) soybean oil*

*1 small zucchini or yellow squash
1 celeriac
1 carrot
2 scallions
olive oil
3 dl (1 1/4 cups) whipping cream
2 tablespoons tarragon
salt and freshly ground pepper
3 tablespoons chopped chives*

SMOKING: Place fish fillets in a large dish and sprinkle with salt and sugar in an even layer. Refrigerate at least 4 hours. Carefully rinse off salt and sugar. Cut the fish into even diagonal slices. Arrange wood chips in the bottom of a pan/pot with a lid. Place a rack over the wood chips. Place over high heat and turn on the exhaust fan. When smoke starts billowing out of the pan, remove from the heat, place fish on the rack, cover, and smoke the fish around 3 minutes. Purchased smoked trout also can be used in this recipe.

MARINATING: Melt the brown sugar in a saucepan. Add tomato puree, soy sauce and tarragon vinegar. Season with pepper sauce, salt and pepper. Brush fish well with the marinade and let marinate about 1 hour.

SAUCE: Peel and coarsely chop the shallots. Sauté in oil until shiny but not brown. Add wine and reduce until about 1/3 of the original amount remains. Beat in butter in pats. Season with salt and pepper. Transfer to a food processor and add the cress. Puree.

VEGETABLES: Thinly slice the eggplant and deep-fry in soybean oil. Drain on paper towels. Set aside. wash and trim the other vegetables and cut into cubes. Sauté in olive oil until soft. Add cream and simmer until thickened. Season with vinegar, salt and pepper. Fold in chives.

FISH: Fry the smoked fish in a little olive oil. Remove from the heat when almost done and let it finish cooking with residual heat.

TO SERVE: Arrange a bed of creamed vegetables on each of four heated plates. Top with fish. Spoon sauce all around and garnish with fresh herbs. Place deep-fried eggplant slices on top.

Salmon Schnitzel with Oyster Tartar
- 4 servings -

600 g (1 1/3 lbs) center-cut salmon fillet

6 oysters
2 tablespoons chopped chives
walnut oil
juice of 1 lemon
salt and freshly ground white pepper

Sauce:
4 shallots
olive oil
1/8 teaspoon saffron
3 dl (1 1/4 cups) fish stock
3 dl (1 1/4 cups) dry white wine
100 g (3 1/2 oz, scant 1/2 cup) unsalted butter, softened
salt and pepper
1/4 tablespoon saffron

3 egg yolks
1 tablespoon Dijon mustard
2 tablespoons whipped cream

chervil

Sauce: Peel and coarsely chop the shallots. Sauté in olive oil with the saffron until shiny but not brown. Add fish stock and wine. Reduce until 1/3 of original amount remains. Beat in the butter in pats. Season with salt and pepper.

While the sauce is cooking, cut the salmon into even squares (schnitzels). Cut a large pocket in the middle of each. Preheat the oven to 200C (400F). Cut salmon trimmings and oysters into small dice and combine with chopped chives. Season with walnut oil, lemon juice, salt and pepper. Stuff each pocket with 1/4 of the tartar. Place on a greased baking sheet. Brush the fish with walnut oil and sprinkle with salt and pepper. Bake 5-10 minutes, according to thickness.

Reheat the sauce. Pour into a food processor with the egg yolks and puree. Season with mustard. Just before serving, fold in the whipped cream.

To serve: Arrange salmon on four heated dinner plates. Pour over sauce. Serve with steamed vegetables and boiled almond potatoes.

Pastry Layers with Jarlsberg Cheese and Marinated Tomatoes with Basil

– 4 servings –

2 sheets frozen puff pastry

Vegetables:
4 large tomatoes
1 can peeled tomatoes
3 drops Louisiana hot pepper sauce
salt and freshly ground white pepper
2 tablespoons chopped chives
2 tablespoons chopped shallots

Basil sauce:
1 large bunch fresh basil
1 1/2 dl (2/3 cup) chicken stock
1 1/2 dl (2/3 cup) mild olive oil
salt and freshly ground pepper

200 g (7 oz) Jarlsberg cheese
100 g (3 1/2 oz) smoked Jarlsberg cheese
fresh basil, salt and pepper

Defrost puff pastry 15 minutes. Preheat the oven to 200C (400F). Roll out and prick with a fork. Place on a parchment-lined baking sheet and bake 15-20 minutes until crispy and golden. Cool and cut into 4x6 cm (1 1/4 x 2 1/4 in) rectangles.

Vegetables: Cut an "x" at the stem end of each tomato. Dip in boiling water about 30 seconds. Transfer immediately with a slotted spoon to ice water. Peel and quarter. Remove seeds with a spoon and puree (the seeds and juice, not the tomatoes themselves) in a food processor with the canned tomatoes. Bring to a boil. Season with pepper sauce, salt and pepper. Combine with the quartered tomatoes. Stir in chives and shallots.

Basil sauce: Blanch basil leaves in boiling water a few seconds. Transfer immediately with a slotted spoon to ice water. Drain. Puree in a food processor with the chicken stock. With the motor running, add olive oil in a thin stream. Puree until bright green. Season with salt and pepper.

Preheat the oven-grill. Cut both types of cheese into 1/2 cm (1/4 in) slices the same size as the pastry rectangles. Place on a parchment-covered baking sheet. Sprinkle with finely chopped basil, salt and pepper. Place under the grill for a few seconds. Carefully heat the vegetable mixture.

To serve: Layer puff pastry squares with the warm vegetable mixture and both kinds of Jarlsberg cheese on four dishes. Drizzle basil sauce all around. These also can be garnished with deep-fried shredded parsley root.

Smoked Salmon Cream with a Salad and Vegetables
- 4 servings -

300 g (10 oz) smoked salmon
1/2 dl (3 tablespoons) whipping cream
50 g (3 tablespoons) unsalted butter, softened
1 dl (scant 1/2 cup) creme fraiche or dairy sour cream (do not use low-fat)
2 tablespoons chopped fresh tarragon
freshly ground white pepper and salt (optional)

Salad/Vegetables:
A mixture of lettuce leaves, such as curly endive, red and green lollo
4 fresh asparagus
2 carrots
2 parsley roots
2 tomatoes

Dressing:
1/2 dl (3 tablespoons) olive oil
4 tablespoons (1/4 cup) balsamic vinegar
1 tablespoon chopped chives
1 tablespoon Dijon mustard

5 dl (2 cups) soybean oil
1 package poppadums (Indian crispbread)

Cut salmon into chunks and place in a food processor. Add cream, butter and creme fraiche and puree until smooth. Press through a sieve and season with tarragon, pepper and, if necessary, a little salt.

Salad/Vegetables: Wash lettuce leaves. Tear into small pieces. Place in a bowl. Clean/peel vegetables and cut into chunks. Parboil in lightly salted water. Plunge into cold water. Drain.

Dressing: Combine all ingredients in a food processor, then pour over vegetables and salad. Toss lightly.

Garnish: Heat the oil in a deep-fryer. Cut poppadums into strips and fry until they float and turn golden. Drain on paper towels.

To serve: Place a mound of smoked salmon cream in the center of 4 dinner plates. Build up with lettuce and vegetables. Top with poppadum strips. Serve with herb dressing or vinaigrette with sesame seeds.

Smoked Salmon with Fried Quail Eggs and Mustard Sauce
– 4 servings –

600 g (1 1/3 lbs) smoked salmon
8 quail eggs
butter
A mixture of lettuce leaves, shredded
2 tablespoons creme fraiche/dairy sour cream

Sauce:
2 egg yolks
1 tablespoon Dijon mustard
1 tablespoon whole grain Dijon mustard
2 dl (3/4 cup) soybean oil
1 tablespoon tarragon vinegar
2 tablespoons chopped fresh tarragon
salt and freshly ground white pepper
water

Sauce: Beat egg yolks and both types of mustard in a food processor. With the motor running, gradually add oil in a thin stream. Be careful that the mixture does not separate. Once all oil is emulsified, the mixture will thicken. Season with vinegar, salt and pepper. Stir in fresh tarragon.

Thinly slice smoked salmon and arrange on four dinner plates. The salmon should cover the entire plate. Fry quail eggs "sunny side up" in butter and place in the center with shredded lettuce all around. Spoon mustard sauce into a small pastry tube and pipe over the salmon. Repeat with creme fraiche/sour cream. Garnish with fresh herbs. Serve with homemade bread.

Dried Meats with Jarlsberg Cheese

Choose your favorite dried meats and sausages. Count on around 150 g (5 oz) per person. Place a large wedge of Jarlsberg cheese, as well as a piece of smoked Jarlsberg on a board. Serve with flatbread, lefse and fresh bread.

Side dishes:

Herb Dressing
4 dl (1 2/3 cups) creme fraiche/dairy sour cream (do not use low-fat)
1 tablespoon mayonnaise
2 tablespoons chopped parsley
2 tablespoons chopped chives
1 tablespoon chopped fresh chervil
1/2 tablespoon chopped tarragon
(and/or other fresh herbs)
juice of 1/2 lemon
salt and freshly ground white pepper

Puree all ingredients in a food processor, adding salt and pepper to taste. If too thick, thin with a little milk. Refrigerate at least several hours before serving, so the flavor can develop.

Faun-marinated lingonberries
400 g (7 1/2 dl, 3 1/2 cups) fresh lingonberries
6 tablespoons brown sugar
1 dl (scant 1/2 cup) Faun (or vodka)

Combine all ingredients in a food process or and pulse several times to crush some, but not all, of the berries.

Juniper-Flavored Sour Cream
3 tablespoons water
100 g (1 1/4 dl, 1/2 cup) sugar
10 juniper berries, crushed
4 dl (1 2/3 cups) dairy sour cream
juice of 1 lemon
salt and freshly ground white pepper
2-3 tablespoons gin (optional)

Bring water and sugar to a boil and add the juniper berries. Marinate overnight. Mix in remaining ingredients.

Chocolate Terrine with Plum Compote
- 8 servings -

Sponge base:
4 eggs
100 g (1 1/4 dl, 1/2 cup) sugar
100 g (1 2/3 dl, 2/3 cup) flour
cocoa

Chocolate cream:
230 g (8 oz) milk chocolate
50 g (2 oz, 4 tablespoons) unsalted butter
230 g (8 oz) semi-sweet chocolate
1/2 liter whipping cream

Plum compote:
3 dl (1 1/4 cups) water
3 dl (1 1/4 cups) sugar
500 g (1 lb) plums (preferably Victoria)
cognac or other flavored spirits
2 teaspoons cornstarch stirred into 2 teaspoons cold water

Licorice/anise coulis:
50 g (3 1/2 tablespoons) sugar
50 g (1 3/4 oz) raw licorice (or 4 star anise)
3 tablespoons water

Sponge base: Preheat the oven to 200C (400F). Beat eggs and sugar until light and lemon-colored. Gradually add flour to make a smooth batter. Line a baking sheet with parchment paper. Spread the batter in an even 1 cm (1/2 in) layer over the paper. Bake until just set, about 3 minutes. Watch carefully. It is possible to make a marbled batter by mixing cocoa into half the batter.

Chocolate cream: Break the milk chocolate into small pieces and place in a mixing bowl with 25 g (2 tablespoons) of the butter. Break the semi-sweet chocolate into small pieces and place in another mixing bowl with 25 g (2 tablespoons) of the butter. Bring the cream to a boil. Pour into a 1 liter (quart) measuring cup and pour 5 dl (2 cups) into each bowl. Let the chocolate melt, then whisk each until smooth.

While the chocolate is cooling, line a 1 1/2 liter (6 cups) loaf pan first with plastic wrap, then with the thin sponge base. All sides should be covered with cake. When the chocolate creams are room temperature, pour in layers in the pan. Cover with a layer of sponge, if desired. Refrigerate overnight.

Plum compote: Bring water and sugar to a boil. Halve the plums and discard the pits. Flavor the sugar syrup with cognac or other spirits. Thicken with cornstarch and water. Place the plums in a bowl and pour over sugar syrup. Marinate overnight.

Licorice/anise coulis: Bring all ingredients to a boil and simmer until thickened.

To serve: Cut the cake into slices and place on plates. Top with plums and syrup. Dot with drops of licorice/anise coulis.

WINTER NORWAY
- there where you couldnt imagine...

Masses of white shining snow, ice-topped lakes and trees covered with frost. The thermometer says it's dangerously cold out there. But that doesn't stop Norwegians from going out and enjoying themselves in the winter landscape.

There's a whirl of activity on the hills and trails, and there's laughter coming from the floodlit ski slopes. In the evening, there are torch-lit rides on horse drawn sleighs, and in some places, people sit in partially enclosed boat-shaped sleighs without runners drawn by lively reindeer bucks. Clad in many layers of clothing, Norwegians set out over frozen lakes and open country.

COLD AND DIFFERENT

Here and there, ice fishermen pull up trout from holes in the ice, and ptarmigan are removed from their snares by hunters on skis.

- Were people ever really supposed to live here? ask visitors from places farther south. But the sturdy hunters and farmers who belong here feel otherwise. And when the winter light plays over large expanses of white and on the ice-covered houses, most people feel that Norway is different, exotic and exciting.

THE PACKED LUNCH PEOPLE

And when we go out for a day of skiing, or to the speed skating track, or just to be spectators at the ski jump, the distinctively Norwegian paper-wrapped lunch is always waiting in the backpack. When it's time for a bite, we take out our open-faced cheese or meat sandwiches. Nothing tastes better out in the open air. And they taste their best when a Norwegian wins gold at an important event, whether it's cross-country or downhill skiing, ski jumping or speed skating.

THE WINTER MENU

Because of the long "infertile" winter, many of the best local Norwegian dishes are based on preserved food. Old traditions and techniques were used to preserve our foods. Since food had to be stored, that requirement determined some of the distinctive Norwegian food and flavor culture. What would the Norwegian kitchen be without good cured ham, fermented or warm-smoked trout, dried reindeer or dried fish and dried salted fish?

For the people living along our chilly coasts, seasonal fishing is important - the fish which will become Christmas cod, lutefisk, marinated herring for the days between Christmas and the new year, or halibut for a special occasion are brought on land. As Christmas draws near, slaughtering of livestock becomes the order of the day. Then there's meat for mutton roll and headcheese, Christmas pork ribs and sausage cakes.

And as Advent and Christmas approach. - Now it's good to be inside, says everyone with a smile. This time before Christmas is filled with social occasions, especially the "julebord," a table laden with all the special Christmas dishes - lutefisk or pork ribs, smoked ribs of mutton or fermented fish. This is a way to sample the traditional dishes before of the holiday. But game is also on the menu throughout the holiday season, especially reindeer and moose, but the best is ptarmigan.

Otherwise, winter is a time for hearty soups and rich, steaming stews, dried salted cod and other fish dishes, all depending upon the location.

Name:
   Yngvar Nilsen
DOB:
   February 18, 1958
Present Position:
   Souschef, Annen Etage, Hotel Continental, Oslo. This has led to working at the restaurants of Alain Chapel and Paul Bocuse in France.
Previous Positions:
   6 months as cook at Annen Etage, cook at Tre Kokker, Oslo; sauce chef at Hotel Continental main kitchen; chef at Restaurant Carte Blanche, Smestad Hotel, Oslo.
Awards:
   A number of medals with the Norwegian Culinary Team.

YNGVAR NILSEN
- from elegant Annen Etage (The Second Floor)

Chef Yngvar Nilsen works at Oslo's finest and most famous hotel, Hotel Continental. Its restaurant - Annen Etage - is one of the most elegant in the country. Top-quality French-inspired cuisine is on the menu here.

Your thoughts about food?

Even the simplest food should be well-prepared. But simpler things sometimes need more care and more work in preparation. It's interesting to combine the simple with the more exclusive. I like to use the finest ingredients when they are best. Correct handling is an art.

What about Norwegian products?

The most important thing is to discover and appreciate the best things we have. I like to work with seafood - shellfish and game fish, especially, such as turbot, sole and fresh ocean catfish! Our strawberries and raspberries are the best you can find. But, unfortunately, our otherwise excellent agricultural products tend to arrive on the market either overmature or unripe. This really needs to be corrected.

And what is your favorite dish?

I think fish that I caught myself earlier that same day, simply prepared, with good potatoes and vegetables, is the best. In general, I like the pure flavors of nature.

How would you describe your cooking style?

I stick to classic well-prepared dishes inspired by French cuisine. You can't get better than that.

Why did you choose to become a chef?

I grew up near the sea, close to nature, and I've always been drawn to its wonderful bounty. Fish and game, fruit and vegetables from our own garden inspired me. Now I find it interesting to travel and learn, to be able to work in countries with other cultures, techniques and traditions. The important thing is that Norwegian is good, but you also have to be open-minded.

Any time for other interests?

I use a lot of my free time to learn more about French food and wine. I have to admit that. Otherwise, I like to fish, work in the garden, and I'm interested in sports.

Is there much time to prepare food at home?

No, it's mostly simple stuff. There's seldom much time. Anyway, when I don't have "kitchen duty," I like to eat food others have prepared.

What about the food of the future?

I believe in a simpler concept with purer food. Good fish and shellfish with exceptional sauces will be important components. But good Norwegian dishes, such as lutefisk, fermented trout and smoked mutton ribs, also deserve respect. As a whole, we should become more selective in everything we do.

Roast Ptarmigan Breast and Reindeer Filet with Lingonberry Sauce

– 4 servings –

Sauce:
4 shallots
water
1 teaspoon butter
1 teaspoon chopped fresh thyme
5 dl (2 cups) reindeer stock
1 dl (scant 1/2 cup) Port wine
3 tablespoons unsalted butter, softened
100 g (2/3 cup) lingonberries

Glazed endives:
2 large endives
1 apple
4 sugar lumps
4 cloves
pinch ground nutmeg
salt and pepper
butter
4 dl (1 2/3 cups) orange juice

Sautéed chanterelles:
1 shallot
butter
400 g (14 oz) fresh chanterelles or other mushrooms (preferably wild)
salt and pepper
1 tablespoon minced parsley

2 black salsify roots
1 liter (quart) soybean oil

2 scallions
butter

4 ptarmigan breasts
400 g (14 oz) reindeer strip loin
salt and pepper
1 teaspoon chopped fresh thyme
butter

Sauce: Peel and chop shallots. Combine with butter, water to just cover and thyme and bring to a boil. Simmer until almost all liquid has evaporated. Add stock and wine. Reduce until half the original amount remains. Strain, then beat in the butter in pats. Stir in the lingonberries.

Glazed endives: Preheat the oven to 175C (350F). Halve the endives. Peel, core and thinly slice the apples. Place the slices between the layers of the endives. Arrange in an oven proof dish. Place one sugar cube, one clove, a sprinkle of nutmeg, salt, pepper and a dot of butter on each. Pour over the orange juice. Bake 50 minutes. Pour the cooking juices into a saucepan and reduce until syrupy. Pour over the endives.

Sautéed chanterelles: Peel and chop the shallot. Sauté in butter. Clean the mushrooms and add. Sauté until tender. Season with salt, pepper and chopped parsley.

Deep-fried black salsify: Wash thoroughly. Peel old roots, but just scrub young ones. Thinly slice with a cheese plane. Heat soybean oil in a deep fryer. Fry until crispy and golden. Drain on paper towels.

Trim any fat and membrane from the meat. Season with salt, pepper and thyme and sauté in butter until medium. Let rest 10 minutes before slicing.

Clean the scallions and cut into lengths. Sauté in butter.

To serve: Place an endive half and 1/4 of the mushrooms on each of four dinner plates. Halve each ptarmigan breast and place on the endive. Slice the reindeer strip loin and place over the mushrooms. Garnish with scallions and salsify chips. Spoon sauce all around. Serve with fried almond potatoes.

— 149 —

Ocean Crayfish Soup

– 4 SERVINGS –

20 whole ocean crayfish

SOUP:
2 tablespoons olive oil
2 tablespoons cognac
2 tablespoons Pernod
1 carrot
1/2 onion
1 garlic clove
2 tomatoes
1 1/2 teaspoons tomato paste
10 peppercorns
fresh tarragon stalks
3 whole star anise
1 liter (quart) fish stock
5 dl (2 cups) whipping cream
salt and pepper
2 tablespoons whipped cream

VEGETABLE GARNISH:
1 carrot
1/2 zucchini
50 g (2 oz) snow peas
1 large yellow bell pepper
2 tablespoons butter

Dip the crayfish in boiling water 30 seconds. Remove the tails, shell and reserve.

SOUP: Crush the crayfish shells and heads. Sauté in olive oil in a soup pot. Pour over cognac and Pernod and flambe. Peel and chop carrot, onion, garlic and tomatoes and add. Sauté together, then add tomato paste, peppercorns, stalks from the tarragon (leaves reserved) and star anise. Pour over the stock. Bring to a boil, lower heat and simmer about 10 minutes. Add cream and simmer 20 minutes. Strain into a clean pan, then reduce over high heat until half the original amount remains. Season with salt and pepper. Just before serving, add whipped cream and tarragon leaves.

VEGETABLE GARNISH: Thinly slice the carrot. Cut balls out of the zucchini with a small melon baller. Shred the snow peas. Dip the bell pepper in boiling water or blister the skin under the grill, then peel and clean. Cut into 1 cm (1/2 in) cubes. Blanch all vegetables in lightly-salted water, then drain. Stir the butter into the vegetables. Heat.

Poach the ocean crayfish tails in salted water, about 3 minutes.

TO SERVE: Arrange the vegetables in four soup bowls. Top with crayfish tails. Ladle over the soup. Serve with hearty bread.

Saffron Mussel Tart
– 4 servings –

2 sheets puff pastry
1 egg yolk
coarse salt

2 - 2 1/2 kg (4 1/2 - 5 lbs) fresh mussels
2 shallots
2 garlic cloves
2 tablespoons olive oil
pinch saffron (or tumeric)
1 teaspoon fresh thyme
2 dl (3/4 cup) white wine
5 dl (2 cups) whipping cream
3 tablespoons unsalted butter, softened
3 tablespoons chopped chives
fresh basil

Ratatouille:
4 medium tomatoes
1 shallot
1 garlic clove
1 tablespoon olive oil
salt, pepper, fresh thyme

Preheat the oven to 220C (425F). Halve each puff pastry sheet. Cut a frame in the dough about 1 cm (1/2 in) from the edge. Brush with egg yolk and sprinkle with coarse salt. Bake 15-18 minutes.

Soak the mussels in running cold water. Clean and scrub well. Peel and chop onion and garlic. Sauté in olive oil with saffron and thyme. Add mussels and white wine. Cover and steam until the mussels open, about 5 minutes. (Discard those which do not open.) Remove with a slotted spoon and strain the cooking liquid. Reduce over high heat until about half the original amount remains. Add cream and bring to a boil. Reduce over high heat until slightly thickened. Remove mussels from their shells, but save 8 for garnish.

Carefully hollow out the puff pastry cases so as not to make any holes or cracks. The lid will be used. Place in the center of four dinner plates.

Ratatouille:
Cut an "x" at the stem end of each tomato. Dip in boiling water about 30 seconds. Transfer immediately with a slotted spoon to ice water. Peel, seed and coarsely chop. Chop onion and garlic and combine with tomatoes and olive oil. Season with salt, pepper and thyme. Heat carefully. Spoon some ratatouille in the bottom of each pastry case.

To serve: Beat the soft butter into the sauce in pats and add mussels and chives. Divide the creamed mussels among the pastry cases. Place the lid slightly at an angle. Garnish with mussels in their shells and more ratatouille. Garnish with fresh basil.

Grilled Scallops with Celeriac Puree and Red Wine Sauce
– 4 servings –

12 scallops
1 tablespoon olive oil
salt and pepper

Celeriac puree:
2 medium celeriacs
1 dl (scant 1/2 cup) milk
juice of 1 lemon
5 tablespoons butter
salt and pepper

Sauce:
2 shallots
1/2 garlic clove
3 3/4 dl (1 1/2 cups) red wine
2 dl (3/4 cup) veal or chicken stock
1 tablespoon balsamic vinegar
3 tablespoons butter, softened
salt and pepper

1/2 red bell pepper
oil
salt and pepper

Clean the scallops. Only the white muscle is used. Halve each horizontally. Rub with olive oil and sprinkle with salt and pepper. Grill in a ridged grill pan, only on the cut side. Cover and set aside so they cook through.

Celeriac puree: Peel and slice celeriac. Cut into large dice. Cook with milk and lemon juice until tender. Transfer to a food processor and puree until smooth. Season with butter, salt and pepper.

Sauce: Peel and chop onion and garlic. Combine in a saucepan with red wine, stock and vinegar. Bring to a boil and reduce over high heat until about half the original amount remains. Strain. Beat in softened butter in pats. Season with salt and pepper.

Garnish: Clean and finely dice the bell pepper. Steam in a little oil and season with salt and pepper.

To serve: Reheat the celeriac puree. Place mounds of puree in the center of four dinner plates. Spoon the sauce all around. Arrange the scallops around the sauce. Top each scallop with diced bell pepper. Garnish with fresh chervil leaves.

Grilled Dried Salt Cod with Vichy-Carrots and Bacon

- 4 SERVINGS -

4 pieces pre-soaked dried salt cod (about 220 g, 8 oz each)
oil

WHITE WINE SAUCE:
3 dl (1 1/4 cups) fish stock
3 dl (1 1/4 cups) white wine
100 g (2/3 cup) chopped shallots
2 dl (3/4 cup) whipping cream
50 g (3 tablespoons) unsalted butter, softened
salt and pepper

VICHY-CARROTS:
600 g (6 medium) carrots
1 bottle (3 dl, 1 1/4 cups) soda water
50 g (3 tablespoons) unsalted butter
salt and pepper
1 teaspoon sugar

400 g (14 oz) bacon
butter

SAUCE: Combine stock, wine and shallots and bring to a boil. Reduce over high heat until about half the original amount remains. Add cream and reduce until half the original amount remains. Strain. Beat in the butter in pats. Season with salt and pepper.

VICHY-CARROTS: Peel and thinly slice the carrots. Combine soda water, butter, salt, pepper and sugar in a saucepan. Add the carrots and cook until tender.

Dice the bacon and brown in butter.

Preheat the oven to 200C (400F). Dry the fish well, then rub with oil. Place in a preheated ridged grill pan. Grill so the fish is imprinted with a pretty pattern. Finish in the oven, about 5 minutes. Remove skin before serving.

TO SERVE: Divide the carrots among four dinner plates. Top with the fish. Spoon the white wine sauce all around. Sprinkle with bacon. Serve with boiled potatoes.

HADDOCK STEW

– 4 SERVINGS –

200 g (3 medium) carrots
200 g (1 large) leek
1 onion
200 g (1/2 medium) celeriac
4 dl (1 2/3 cups) fish stock
100 g (3 1/2 oz, scant 1/2 cup) unsalted butter
800 g (1 3/4 lbs) boneless and skinless haddock fillet
salt and pepper
2 dl (3/4 cup) white wine
4 dl (1 2/3 cups) whipping cream
2 tablespoons flour
200 g (7 oz, 7/8 cup) unsalted butter, softened
fresh chervil

Clean and peel vegetables and cut into julienne. Steam in a small amount of the fish stock with butter. Cut the fish into 3x6 cm (1x2 in) chunks. Sprinkle with salt and pepper about 30 minutes before cooking.

Combine fish stock, white wine and cream in a large saucepan. Beat in the flour and bring to a boil, stirring constantly. Reduce over high heat until about half the original amount remains. Beat in the butter in pats. Add the fish and vegetables and heat through.

TO SERVE: Divide among four soup bowls and serve with French bread or boiled potatoes.

Lime Soufflé with Blackberry Sauce

– 4 SERVINGS –

SAUCE:
400 g (14 oz) blackberries
2 dl (3/4 cup) sugar
2 dl (3/4 cup) water
juice of 1/2 lemon

75 g (1/3 cup) sugar
45 g (3 tablespoons) flour
4 egg yolks
4 1/2 dl (1 7/8 cups) milk
juice and zest of 4 limes
butter
sugar

5 egg whites
confectioner's sugar

SAUCE: Bring sugar and water to a boil. Simmer 2 minutes. Cool. Add to a food processor with the berries and puree. Add lemon juice to taste.

Whisk sugar, flour and egg yolks together. Bring milk to a boil. Whisk the milk into the egg yolk mixture and cook until slightly thickened. Strain. Add lime juice and zest. Preheat the oven to 190C (375F). Grease 4 individual soufflé molds with butter and sprinkle with sugar. Beat egg whites until almost stiff. Fold in 1 tablespoon confectioner's sugar. Fold the beaten egg whites into the soufflé mixture. Pour into the soufflé molds. Bake 15-17 minutes. Sprinkle with confectioner's sugar before serving.

TO SERVE: When the soufflés are served, cut into the top of each and pour over the cold sauce.

Register:

17th of May	110
17th of May cake	114
Almond macaroon cake	52
Almond ring cake	56
Anise parfait	118
Autumn tarte	123
Bacalao Superiore	72
Bacon, onion and Jarlsberg Quiche	90
Baked apples in filo	120
Baked dried salt cod with smoked tomatoes	16
Baked halibut	70
Baked halibut with lemon thyme sauce	100
Baked reindeer strip loin with thyme	18
Barbeque-smoked trout	130
Brochettes of salmon and halibut in soy sauce marinade	82
Cappuccino ice cream cake	46
Chocolate terrine with plum compote	142
Cloudberry mousse cake	22
Cod and ocean crayfish pizza	32
Cold rhubarb-strawberry soup	91
Creamy fish and shellfish soup	29
Dried meats with Jarlsberg cheese	140
Dried salt cod pizza	20
Erichsen's nut cake	44
Filet of veal with rosemary and Jarlsberg scalloped potatoes	104
Finnmark	6
Fjord Norway	58
Frank Baer	60
Fruitcake	50
Grilled dried salt cod with vichy-carrots and bacon	156
Grilled marinated salmon with mustard sauce	10
Grilled scallops with celeriac puree and red wine sauce	154
Haddock quenelles with curried Jarlsberg sauce	106
Haddock stew	158
Harald Osa	78
Hearty cod and tomato bouillon	28
Herbed lamb filet with aromatic vegetables	88
Herbed rack of lamb with marinated eggplant	36
Index	160
Jorn Lie	128
Lars Lian	42
Lightly salted and smoked leg of lamb	68
Lightly-salted cod and smoked shrimp with almond potato puree	80
Lime soufflé with blackberry sauce	159
Lofoten	24
Lukewarm Jarlsberg tart	30
Mackerel burgers with cold rhubarb soup	98
Marinated salmon sandwich	66
Nina Sjøen	112
Norwegian cookies	124
Ocean crayfish soup	150
Odd Ivar Solvold	26
Pasjons fruit cheesecake	116
Pasjons fruit mousse	54
Pastry layers with Jarlsberg cheese and marinated tomatoes with basil	134
Pickled mackerel with summer vegetables	96
Pollack and potatoes layered with onion marmalade	34
Roast ptarmigan breast and reindeer filet with lingonberry sauce	148
Rogaland	76
Røros	126
Saffron mussel tart	152
Salad with smoked Jarlsberg cheese and marinated eggplant	102
Salmon burgers with smoked Jarlsberg	62
Salmon schnitzel with oyster tartar	132
Salmon soup with pickled root vegetables	14
Salmon with herb risotto	64
Salt-baked cod with beet sauce	12
Sardines on toast	86
Semi-frozen apple-spice cream with candied apricots	38
Shrimp in their shells with herb sauce and toast	84
Smoked salmon cream with a salad and vegetables	136
Smoked salmon with fried quail eggs and mustard sauce	138
Strawberry cake	48
Sørlandet	92
To lovers of good food everywhere	2
Tor Morten Myrseth	8
Traditional ingredients – Modern food	4
Trond Moi	94
Trøndelag	40
Veiled southern girls	108
Warm cherries with red wine sauce and cinnamon ice cream	74
Warm chocolate tart with coconut sauce	122
Winter Norway	144
Yngvar Nilsen	146

Mainphoto: 6, 110 – Husmofoto
Photo: Top/bottom 7, topp 111 – Husmofoto
Mainphoto: 24, 76, 92, 144 – Per Eide
Photo: Middle/bottom 25, bottom 41, bottom 59, middle 77, middle 93 – Per Eide